Barcode on Book

S0-BQY-654

HUMBER LIBRARIES LAKESHORE CAMPUS
3199 Lakeshore Blvd West
TORONTO, ON.   M8V 1K8

DISCARD

LOCAVORE

FROM FARMERS' FIELDS
TO ROOFTOP GARDENS

. . .

LOCAVORE

. . .

HOW CANADIANS ARE
CHANGING THE WAY WE EAT

SARAH ELTON

HarperCollins*Publishers*Ltd

HUMBER LIBRARIES LAKESHORE CAMPUS
3199 Lakeshore Blvd West
TORONTO, ON. M8V 1K8

Locavore
Copyright © 2010 by Sarah Elton.
All rights reserved.

Published by HarperCollins Publishers Ltd.

No part of this book may be used or reproduced in any manner whatsoever
without the prior written permission of the publisher, except in the case of
brief quotations embodied in reviews.

HarperCollins books may be purchased for educational, business,
or sales promotional use through our Special Markets Department.

HarperCollins Publishers Ltd
2 Bloor Street East, 20th Floor
Toronto, Ontario, Canada
M4W 1A8

www.harpercollins.ca

Library and Archives Canada Cataloguing in Publication

Elton, Sarah, 1975–
Locavore : from farmers' fields to rooftop gardens—how Canadians are
changing the way we eat / Sarah Elton.

ISBN 978-1-55468-418-2

1. Local foods–Canada. 2. Food habits–Canada.
3. Farm produce–Canada. I. Title.

TX360.C3E48 2009   641.300971   C2009-905747-6

Printed and bound in Canada

DWF 9 8 7 6 5 4 3 2 1

for Kumail

CONTENTS

LOCAL FOOD FOR CANADA

I t all started with a cookie. A bakery cookie decorated with sugary pink icing to look like a pig. It reminded me of the treats my grandmother used to buy for me and my sister. My elder daughter brought the pink cookie home in a loot bag along with some bath paints and dollar-store toys. I was going to let her eat it, until I flipped it over and read the sticker on the back of the shrink-wrapped package. There, at the end of a long list of ingredients, was something I was more surprised to see than soy lecithin and artificial colouring. This cookie was no ordinary bakery confectionery. No, this cookie was made—I gasped—in China. I knew my shoelaces were made in China, the light switches in my house were made in China, and the shovel in my backyard and most of my clothing too. But this was a cookie, not a pair of pants; an item of food imbued with all sorts of cultural associations with home, happiness and family.

Rather than having been baked where I'd expected, in a bakery, this cookie was created in a Chinese factory, run by an American company that makes six million of them every year. When I later called their headquarters, I learned that this cookie's journey to my house began on a 175-foot-long conveyor belt from where it was loaded into a transport truck to be taken to a distant port and loaded again into the cargo hold of a ship that would take three weeks to travel to Vancouver from where it would be driven by yet another truck across the Rockies, the Prairies, around Lake Superior, south of Sault Ste. Marie, to Sudbury, and finally to Toronto. This cookie had a carbon load of a coal-fired power station.

This innocuous-looking pink-iced thing spurred me on a quest to understand more about the foods we eat and where they come from, and in the process changed the way I eat and the way I feed my family of four.

For some reason, that cookie brought it all together for me: everything that was wrong with our long-distance food system was embodied in that sugary pink pig. Until then, I could accept a supermarket where, all year round, you could find the same products, like Californian salad-in-a-bag, South African fruit juice medley, and New Zealand lamb. I hadn't questioned the bananas that sat in our fruit bowl or thought much about our daily dose of orange juice. I shopped and ate just like most other people in North America. I think the reason the cookie was the tipping point for me was because it was something that could easily have been made in Canada—an iced cookie isn't exactly a mango or a starfruit, something exotic from the tropics. And not only could this cookie have been made here, but had it been, it would have been an intrinsically better cookie. Had it been baked that morning in a local bakery to be sold to someone to eat that same day, it would have been fresh. It would not have required a mile-long ingredients list and, likely, it would have been an altogether tastier and, I'll hazard to say, healthier cookie.

Wait a minute, I thought. If this benign-looking cookie was made in China—and I only happened to catch sight of its origins written in minuscule print on the back of the wrapper—what other surprises could I find in my grocery cart? Being a journalist with a food column simplified the task of uncovering what other products were being made in China for North American consumption. After a few phone calls, I learned that virtually all our apple juice and fruit juice medleys, such as cranberry cocktail and grape juice, contain concentrate made from apples grown in one of China's thousand-acre apple orchards; that China is the number one grower of pears, asparagus and black beans, and that the country produces more and more tomatoes for processing into paste and sauces every year. According to one business report out of China, more than half of the fruits and vegetables grown on planet Earth are cultivated there, not just to feed the populous nation but to supply its rapidly expanding agricultural export industry. China is producing more and more of our food.

The ecological ramifications of buying food grown as far away as China are enormous—not to mention the implications of relying on a country with a shoddy record of protecting consumers from tainted foods. I immediately started asking myself, what was the environmental cost of this long-distance food chain? China, of course, isn't the only country participating in industrial export agriculture, so what other distant countries were supplying major components of my diet here in Canada? And if China was now growing most of the apples for our juices, vast quantities of sunflower seeds and tomatoes and fill-in-the-blanks that Canadian farmers grow here too, what was happening to the men and women in our country whose livelihoods depended on farming? What was the fate of the farmland they cultivated? It was somewhere between my kitchen and the grocery store that the connection between the food we eat in Canada and serious environmental problems such as climate change, the ecological toll of industrial agriculture and the future of our food supply became startlingly obvious. The geographical distance our food travels, I realized, was a metaphor for the true environmental cost of our food.

I might live in the country's biggest city and far away from farmers' fields, but it's the same story across Canada. No matter how close you live to farmland, chances are the food you are eating travelled long distances. In Newfoundland, less than 10 percent of the food people eat is grown on the island. In Quebec, imports crowd the shelves. A 2005 study conducted by FoodShare in Toronto found that food in a sample shopping basket from a downtown grocery store travelled an average distance of 5,364 kilometres. In Manitoba, despite its strong agricultural sector, most of what you'll find in people's kitchens comes from elsewhere. And on Vancouver Island, where only a few decades ago a resident's diet was made up of 85 percent locally grown and processed foods, this number has plummeted to less than 10 percent. Despite the emergence on the mainstream stage of the lively local-food movement, which has given us a wonderful network of farmers' markets, Community Supported Agriculture schemes and other ways to buy local food, we continue to import the very same foods we actually grow here—and then export what we produce. Carrots from Ontario's richest soils, in the Holland Marsh, are loaded onto trucks and driven south to the United States and shipped to places as far away as Puerto Rico and Venezuela, passing other trucks heading north loaded with American carrots destined for Ontario stores.

And it's not just carrots. We import all sorts of fruits and vegetables into Canada that we cultivate right here. According to data collected by Statistics Canada, much of the broccoli we eat comes from the United States, followed by Mexico and China. We import lettuce primarily from the United States and Mexico, but we also fly it in from China despite the fact that air travel is the most carbon-heavy form of shipping. We truck in potatoes from the United States even though, according to the United Potato Growers of Canada, farmers in Prince Edward Island in 2008 and 2009 grew 907 million kilograms of the tubers. The way we Canadians eat is simply not sustainable.

What all these facts and figures meant for me as a consumer was that every choice I made at the grocery store was suffused with larger issues and had implications not only for our family's pocketbook and our health but for the future of the planet—a pretty dire pronouncement for a regular old grocery run. I would find myself stumped in the produce aisle: organic or local? In the cooler section I'd ponder which was better, the really expensive organic milk or the regular stuff for less than half the price, all the while shivering in front of open refrigerated shelves of milk. What was the environmental cost of *that*? Should I switch to a grocer who kept the milk behind glass doors, thus using less energy to keep it chilled? Then there were my kids' favourite crackers. The label reads that they are made in the United States but doesn't indicate where each of the ingredients originates. Were the milk solids made in New Zealand? Were the soybeans pressed for the oil grown in Brazil on Amazon rainforest recently cleared to sow this highly profitable legume?

The processed foods in our modern supermarket are an amalgam of ingredients sourced on the global marketplace, which means that I, as a consumer, can't know where each of the components was grown, how they were processed and what kind of journey they've taken from the field all the long way to my plate. So I muddled around, trying to figure out what purchasing decisions I was comfortable with as a mother and as a citizen. Before I knew there was a word for it, I had become a locavore.

I'm now a twenty-first-century urban hunter-gatherer. There is an abundance of food in my neighbourhood—I live on the east side of Toronto's downtown, three blocks from one of the city's several Chinatowns and within a kilometre of three big chain supermarkets. I can drive a short distance to Indian stores and Afghan grocers, and walk to cheese shops, high-end butchers and small bakeries. And yet, as a locavore, I must search out the local food. Every few months, I travel several kilometres to a small store that sells meat from animals raised by Mennonites in Southern Ontario. I love the bread at the bakery that uses flour grown and milled in the province, so I pick up my loaves there. A mom-and-pop fruit and vegetable stand on the main street in my neighbourhood stocks a variety of local produce that they purchase at the Ontario Food Terminal. My dad supplies me with potatoes from his country garden and, depending on the success of the harvest, with beets, carrots and onions, and I go to the farmers' markets and the independent grocery store that specializes in organic foods to buy other veggies but also for the really special stuff like Jerusalem artichokes and tomatillos. I do shop at the big-box store and buy some processed foods (the kids love those cheesy crackers) and a moderate amount of tropical produce like oranges and bananas in the winter for my children and husband. Besides, I am a global eater; I have no nostalgia for the pioneer diet and enjoy my chicken tikka and pad Thai. So I keep my kitchen stocked with cardamom, rice and olive oil. In the colder months, I even buy the odd organic Californian broccoli, particularly in March when the local food provisions I'd squirrelled away run out and there isn't much else green that is grown nearby. But to every trip to the store, I bring a locavore's mindset: if you can grow it here, I won't buy it from there. That one pink cookie profoundly changed my relationship to food.

·

The cookie epiphany aside, my interest in local foods, farming and sustainable living is a predictable path in my life. My parents raised me to be just like this, to think about the big issues, to care about the natural world and to take pleasure in watching the seeds sprout. My dad is an avid grower of his own food and an environmentalist who feels an almost transcendental connection to the earth. He and my mother did their best to expose my sister and me to nature, even though we grew up in downtown Toronto. In my childhood home, there was an orange tree in the dining room that produced a biannual harvest of tiny fruit the size of golf balls. They were sour enough to make your mouth pucker but with a flavour so light and delicate that I'd suck their pulp anyway. At a young age, I was well versed in the process of pollination and, lacking insects indoors to do the job, I'd use a paintbrush to transfer the pollen from stamen to pistil. Scattered about the place were copies of back-to-the-earth magazines like *Mother Earth News* and *Harrowsmith,* to which my dad subscribed. The stories of homesteading hippies raising chickens and goats in Northern British Columbia had me imagining what it would be like to live off the land, milking my own goats each morning, going to the root cellar for potatoes in the cold winter, just like Laura Ingalls in *Little House on the Prairie*. At my grandparents' farm, we'd cut fresh stalks of asparagus, pull carrots, play tag with the cousins in the corn rows and come home from an autumn visit with bags of apples we had picked from the old gnarled trees on the property.

When I was twelve, my parents bought their own farm that we would visit on the weekends. Soon after they took it over, they acquired some cows. I watched the animals range freely on the acreage, eating grass all summer, hay in the winter, until a big truck drove up the driveway and loaded them into the back to be taken to auction. I'd heard about vegetarians decrying the treatment of cows and other farm animals, but based on my experience, cows seemed to have a pretty good life. The cattle on our farm were lucky beasts, I thought. They were free to roam the two hundred acres and eat the grass all day. Some of them didn't venture from the back fields to the barn for weeks at a time, preferring to stay in the shaded areas on the edge of the rear woodlot. If cows lived like that, what was cruel about their treatment? (Of course, I hadn't yet learned of the factory farms from which the vast majority of our meat in North America comes and likely the kind of place the calves from our farm would be sent after we sold them, to be grain-finished—fattened up—before slaughter.)

My dad planted his own vegetable garden, and I remember wondering each spring how the weather and climate that summer would affect the fall crop. One year, the beans did so well we had baskets and baskets of them to eat. Another year, it was the onions that thrived, and they were sweeter than they had ever been. Then one hot summer, it was the tomato plants that produced bushels of fruit. At the farm, we also discovered heritage apple trees, which produced translucents, a white-fleshed apple with a delicate soft yellow skin that made a pink applesauce. All this food discovery was matter-of-fact for me back then. It was a part of life I took for granted, just as any child or young person would, not realizing that their experience is shaped by personal circumstance.

Then I grew up and forgot all about this way of interacting with the world. As a young adult, I preferred to travel to places like India, Guatemala and Italy rather than heading to the backwoods. Besides, I loved living in the city, as downtown as possible; most of the time, the thicket of high-rises near my apartment was the closest I'd get to a forest. Periodically, I'd embark on some project that would reconnect me with the natural world and the places where our food originates. I spent the summer after first-year university volunteering on organic farms in British Columbia, where I learned how to milk a cow by hand, fork hay into the barn for winter forage and move irrigation pipes from field to field. On my parents' farm, which I visited regularly, I would collect fruit from the wild apple trees and pick the mint that grew on the banks of the stream to dry for wintertime tea, keeping me, at least partially, connected to the food loop. And during university, I joined a food co-op and started to learn about the benefits of organic agriculture. But in hindsight, I see that every year I grew a little more distant from the origins of my food, from the land that produces it and the environment that sustains the whole system.

Fast-forward a decade or so. I gave birth to a baby girl during a February snowstorm that just about shut down the city. Holding this tiny being for the first time awakened me to a connection with the past and to the future, woke me up to the generational arc of life. After the blur of the first six months of motherhood, I started to yearn for the natural world. I wanted my daughter to experience the same connection to nature that my father had cultivated in me. As a parent, I understood the richness of experience my parents had offered me in providing me with the chance to know that asparagus looks, to a child, like a green Martian rocket ship when it shoots out of the ground. A chance to be familiar with the sound of a cow munching on grass. To know that the grass the cow's giant tongue, extending from its mouth in an almost circular motion, pulls into its jaws will one day, indirectly, become my own dinner. That applesauce is made at home, not in a factory, and that fresh vegetables taste really good in a homemade soup.

When thinking about how to foster this connection for my elder daughter first, and then for my second baby when she was born two and a half years later, I realized that mine had been ruptured by the simple fact that I lived in a major Canadian city where opportunities to commune with one's food are few. The industrial food system that brings most of us our food, distances the consumer from the farm. Its factory efficiency has ensured that everything in the supermarket looks as if humans, not nature, made it. The sanitized, giant chicken breasts, without feathers, blood or any other trace of their avian origins; lemons so shiny and yellow they look as if they are made of plastic; broccoli heads without the worms of my youth (my mom called them protein). I needed to reinstate this connection, not just for my daughters but for my own sake. Everybody benefits from a deeper understanding of our place in the food chain.

So I planted tomatoes in large plastic pots in the backyard and a selection of brassica greens in a barrel. The first summer I tried to grow tomatoes, I lost my fight with the raccoons, who ate every single fruit just as it ripened. I perfected my tactics the following year by planting only cherry tomatoes, which, for some reason, didn't appeal to the animals. Now my four-year-old loves to go out and hunt for the small red fruit amid the sprawling vines. She dislikes the taste of tomato but permits herself to touch their flesh, to pick and feed them to her younger sister, who eats them like popcorn. The girls also know how to dig potatoes and carrots, which they've learned from my mom and dad. When we pass nasturtium flowers in someone's garden, the older one points them out as edible and good for a salad. I think that even though we live downtown, they will grow up with an understanding of where their food comes from, an appreciation of the incredible cycle of the natural world that we are part of every time we eat.

·

When I think of how different my interactions with food are today from what my grandmother's were when she was raising her two children in the years after the Great Depression and the Second World War, it's hard to believe that such a fundamental cultural change took place in the space of only two generations. Back then, when the North American food system was in the early stages of industrialization, milk was still delivered to the house by a milkman in a horse-drawn cart. He would deposit the glass bottles of unhomogenized milk in a special compartment built into the bricks by the side door—a milk box. My mom remembers what would happen if an Ottawa cold snap got to the milk before she did: the frozen milk would push the cream out of the bottle in the shape of a popsicle. Much of the food her family ate would have been grown locally, likely without chemical pesticides—for the pesticide industry grew out of the war machine when weapons researchers were redirected to agriculture, and DDT, invented for war in the early 1940s, needed a civilian use. The grocery store chain back then was an evolved version of the general store, a small-scale greengrocer that was nothing like the vast modern supermarkets that opened later with the rise of the suburb and the automobile. When my grandmother first became a mother, just after the war, she bought food for the family at the greengrocer as well as at the butcher and the baker, because all the small shops of an old-fashioned main street were still prevalent. In Canada it was possible then to buy bananas and oranges as well as other fruits that had been shipped north; in the early twentieth century, iceberg lettuce was already transported over long distances in refrigerated railcars. The selection at the store was nothing like the season-less produce section of today's supermarket, and when you did buy an orange, it was special. In our house, we still put an orange in our Christmas stockings, a holdover from a time when tropical fruit was an exciting treat.

Food preparation didn't resemble what I do in my kitchen either. When my grandmother bought her first electric stove, the salesman taught her to turn off the dial and wait for the residual heat to do the final cooking so as not to waste electricity. My grandmother had a fridge in Canada, but her family back in England didn't—the majority of the population there didn't refrigerate their foods till the 1970s, around the time I was born. And even though my grandmother's fridge had a freezer, every summer she rushed with a squirrel's instinct to preserve the harvest with her jams and fruit leathers.

Just as my experiences today are different from hers, my children's will likely be equally as different from my own, because by the time they are adults, whether we like it or not our food system will probably not resemble what it is today. In fact, if we want to maintain a good quality of life while living within our ecological means, then our food system *must* change. Many things are wrong with the current system. Abundant, cheap calories in processed foods have created an enormous health burden by feeding an obesity epidemic and pushing up diabetes rates worldwide. The food security of states has been compromised because many countries are no longer able to feed themselves without relying on imports—what would happen if some political or security crisis were to shut down national borders or a natural disaster interrupted trade routes? Then there's the general absence of deliciousness in the food produced by the industrial system; qualities like durability in transit have priority over taste, and simultaneous ripening times are considered more valuable than genetic diversity. But the industrial food complex deal breaker for me is the environmental cost of our food system.

The way we eat today is not sustainable. In the years since the Second World War, we have industrialized the practice of farming around the world and created a polluting food system that is dependent on fossil fuels. On the farm, we use machines powered by oil and gas, instead of human muscle and horses, to work the land and to irrigate it too. The good news is that technology has allowed farmers to reap high returns per hour of labour they spend in the fields, which has meant a huge improvement in standard of living for all of us. We've been freed as a society from the drudgery and poverty of subsistence farming that was the reality of life for many Canadians over the centuries. A farmer today is able to produce, per hour of labour, 350 times more than a First Nations farmer would have on the same North American soils.[1] To live free from subsistence farming is undeniably a good thing. However, to support this way of farming, we use natural gas to make fertilizer to treat the soil so we can plant the vast monocultures—only one crop planted over acres and acres—that epitomize large-scale agriculture. These monocrops are more susceptible to pests, so we then make pesticides from oil to kill the insects. Then we continue to use our precious resources to irrigate, transport and process the crops.

North American agriculture requires more groundwater than can be replenished naturally—so we're operating at a 25 percent overdraft.[2] The way we farm is also depleting the soil. We are losing topsoil eighteen times faster than it is being replaced. Because we are not taking care of the soil's health, farmers have had to abandon formerly fertile land that has been exhausted by agriculture; in some of the most productive farming areas, soil fertility has been reduced by 50 percent. The only reason we've been able to maintain the high yields is because we employ fossil fuels to make pesticides and fertilizers.

The way we raise livestock also has a devastating effect on the environment. Cattle, pigs, sheep and chickens, when raised in the intensive operations of the industrial food system, eat significant resources in the form of their feed. They require large quantities of water to survive, and then, because we keep them in such huge numbers, their waste becomes a toxic sludge that we don't know what to do with. In addition, according to the Food and Agriculture Organization of the United Nations, the livestock industry around the world accounts for at least 18 percent of humanity's greenhouse gas emissions.

And now that food is no longer sold and eaten near to where it was grown or processed, we needlessly use energy to transport what could have been produced nearby. When we grow food in one place and ship it, fly it, truck it and send it by rail from one country to another, one continent to the next, one hemisphere to the other, we burn fossil fuels, depleting this earth's non-renewable energy stores and also releasing carbon dioxide, a harmful greenhouse gas, into the atmosphere, thus contributing to climate change. Today we are using more kilocalories to grow and move the food than there are kilocalories in the food itself. Each kilocalorie we consume has taken ten kilocalories to produce, process and ship. David Pimentel, a professor of ecology and agricultural sciences at Cornell University who has published more than six hundred scientific articles and sat on the National Academy of Sciences, calculated that it takes 1,514 litres of oil to feed the average North American.[3] That's 1,514 litres of ancient solar energy that has been stored for thousands of years and that is now gone forever. To eat in a sustainable way, we must gain more calories from the food than the calories consumed to make it.

The scientists who study climate change are now predicting that we have only twenty years left to act. We must dramatically reduce our emissions and lessen our impact on this planet, otherwise we will have passed the point of no return. Already, much of the Arctic ice cap has melted and the rate of melting of the Greenland ice sheet has soared. World-renowned scientist Tim Flannery, who chairs the Copenhagen Climate Council and whose rallying cries around climate change have brought the issue to the political fore in his native Australia and drawn attention to it here in Canada, warns that soon we as a species will have so altered our climate that it will never be the same. Once we pass that point of no return, humanity will live in an uncertain world.

These dramatic declarations make it hard to imagine what difference an individual could possibly make. However, once you understand the connection between the food choices you make and the environment, you can help start to change the system. Food is a personal issue and is something we engage with every day. By making consumer choices that support the creation of a sustainable local food economy, we are helping to create solutions that may lead us out of this environmental morass. Perhaps this is why the local-food movement has had such widespread appeal in Canada and around the world.

•

But is it possible to develop a local food system in Canada? Many people argue that we have no choice but to import food to sustain our large population in a country where the temperature drops below zero for a good portion of the year. We may grow wheat and raise good beef, but we need to supplement our diet with food we bring in from elsewhere, they suggest. Canada is not Italy or even the United States with its swaths of southern land. Local food is impossible for us, hold the naysayers.

On the contrary. A local and sustainable food system *is* possible in Canada. We can feed ourselves—and with good food at that—in this great expanse of northerly land. This doesn't mean returning to lives of subsistence agriculture or eating only turnips, potatoes and onions for months on end. Advances in technology and agriculture mean we can create a whole new way of growing and distributing food that is sustainable. Nor does shifting to local food in Canada mean embracing the 100-mile diet. Despite the prevalent belief that food grown closer to where it is eaten is better for the environment, food miles are *not* the best way to measure sustainability. In fact, it can often take fewer kilocalories to grow food and ship it great distances to where it is eaten than it takes for a local farmer to truck food to a nearby market. Because local doesn't trump sustainable, the way we grow our food in Canada therefore must change too.

When the term *locavore* was coined in 2005 in San Francisco to describe someone who subsists on foods grown and produced nearby, it captured the feelings of a generation that was awakening to the fact that the price they were paying at the supermarket didn't reflect the true cost of their food. The term had such resonance that it spread beyond the burgeoning local-food movement and was quickly adopted into the popular lexicon. In 2007, the *Oxford American Dictionary* declared it "word of the year." Five years after *locavore* came to be, the debate around food has become more nuanced, and the idea of local food encapsulates more than simply geography. The local-food movement today advocates for food that is produced in a way that has the least impact on the environment. It's about recalibrating the number of kilocalories we use to make the food against the number of kilocalories we can extract from it. The term *foodshed* is often used to describe an ecological region in which food is grown and consumed. The concept is not unlike that of a watershed and describes a natural balance that the local-food movement advocates for.

We don't have to abandon coffee, chocolate and spices to support a new food system. Rather, the ideal of a strong local food economy is to eat good, healthy food that is produced with the least environmental impact. This usually means food that is produced nearby, but includes imports that are produced and transported sustainably. For this reason, people like Will Allen, an urban-agriculture guru in Milwaukee, are starting to call the efforts to transform today's food system "the good food revolution."

There is so much to gain from building a local food system in Canada, and there is so much more to lose by not acting immediately. We must learn to feed ourselves without destroying the planet. If we don't start creating an alternative to Californian strawberries in January and Mexican tomatoes in March, then we could be in for an unpleasant surprise. Already we know that new and extreme weather patterns caused by climate change will affect our ability to grow our food; in fact, it's already happening. Drought in some parts of the world is devastating crops, while storms cause extreme flooding in other regions. If turbulent weather or a severe drought caused grain or rice crops to fail around the world, millions of us would starve. We need to create sustainable local food systems to ensure that we can all feed ourselves delicious and healthy foods into the future.

The good news is that there are people out there right now piecing together this new system in every province. *Locavore* tells the stories of how chefs, gardeners, farmers, young people, old people, urbanites, rural foodies, gourmets and regular folk are creating a new way of growing food and putting it on the table. These people are your local cheese maker, the artisan baker down the way, the farmer who sells you eggs, the woman who works part-time at the bookstore so she can volunteer to run the neighbourhood farmers' market, your friend from university who left a job in the city to make a go of it on her own organic farm, the chef at the nearby restaurant who features local farm fare on her menu—the thousands and thousands of Canadians who inspire us with their new and exciting approaches to food. So many people I have spoken with while researching this book know a local hero they wanted me to meet. While you may not find your particular hero in the pages of this book, you will meet many people who are not unlike those you know and who are working towards the same goal.

Each of the book's parts looks at the two halves of the food equation. We start on the farm, where food originates, and then in Part Two travel to the city that needs to be fed and increasingly must find ways to feed itself. This book documents my journey along the food chain to witness how the pieces of this new local food system are coming together and to catch a glimpse of a future that is good both for us and for the planet too.

It's a hopeful story that doesn't dwell on our mistakes but rather demonstrates that change is possible and that our problems are surmountable.

When you finish this book, hopefully you too will feel as optimistic about the future as I do, armed with the knowledge to make the food choices that will help to create a new food order. And with each meal you eat, you too will feel that you are making a difference.

PART ONE

. . .

ON
THE
FARM

CHAPTER ONE

FARMING FOR THE FUTURE
The Fall and Rise of the Family Farm in New Brunswick

The road to Acadieville runs ruler straight, north west from Moncton. The drive to this small town in southeastern New Brunswick follows the old CN Rail line and is a one-hour trip up a now desolate Highway 126. Not that long ago, the road shot through beautiful farm country; these days there's not much to be seen from the car window other than a few houses, a post office and a whole lot of brush. The turn-off for Acadieville is marked by a small sign. Once you've made the turn, you wind your way through the village that stretches eastward, modest houses strung along the side of the road like rosary beads, leading to the old Acadian church. Across the way from its towering white wooden steeple is the home of Donald and Viola Daigle. Their farmhouse has been the headquarters of the Really Local Harvest Co-op—or, as they call it here in Acadian country where most people speak French first, English second, La Récolte de Chez-Nous—an organization founded by a group of local farmers that has transformed the rural reality here.

These days, the sound of hammers dominates at Donald and Viola's house. Donald recently stepped down as executive director and chair of the co-op, a position he's held since shortly after its inception in 2000.

After so many years of putting their own projects on hold, Donald and Viola are taking the time to improve their house. It's an old farmhouse with white clapboard siding, slanting floors and a wood-fired furnace in the basement to keep the place warm in the cold winters that strike these parts. They're replacing the old, drafty windows and all the doors too, installing a new washroom, building an attached garage and covering the house with siding. Their upgrades are overdue, but it has been decades since there has been the extra money for work like this. None of the renovations would likely have been possible had the Daigles not joined the Really Local Harvest Co-op.

Donald is a slender man, spry, with the energy of a border collie. He wears his greying brown hair short, has a moustache, and his eyebrows have grown a little wild with age. At fifty-two, he's a father of five, a keen business man and a successful vegetable farmer who grows what he calls "simple foods" like Brussels sprouts, broccoli, cauliflower, turnips, carrots, cabbages and potatoes. His French is Acadian, sprinkled with English-French hybrids like "Tu me callera" and old expressions such as, translated loosely, "If your bare foot feels good walking in the dirt, then the soil is good for planting." He often finishes sentences in English with a French *la*. As in, "To me, a day without potatoes is a sad day, *la*." He drives a big grey pickup truck with wheels so high that heaving myself into the cab takes as much effort as saddling a horse.

Viola works alongside Donald, supporting all the farm activities, making deliveries, keeping the books. She is a small woman with her hair worn in a pixie cut that makes her look too young to be the mother of five almost-grown children. When Donald chose to dedicate his time to building the co-op, it meant he committed his family's resources too, and Viola was right there beside him. She understood that they were creating something special. She could see that, unless they as a family, as a farm and as a farming community changed along with the new reality of the globalized marketplace, they would become dinosaurs, frozen in time.

Donald was raised in Acadieville and has seen drastic change come to this small town. As a child, life here wasn't much different for Donald than it would have been for his father and his father's father before that. Things had remained pretty much the same since his ancestors arrived in the area in 1685 after having been expelled from Nova Scotia by the British. His large Acadian family—he has fourteen brothers and sisters—was more or less self-sufficient. They kept a cow for milk, chickens for eggs, pigs and lambs for meat, and they grew some vegetables too. Donald's mother, in addition to taking care of the many children, prepared all the food, including the butter and bread, and knitted socks and mittens and blankets for everyone from the wool of their sheep. Every Saturday, she baked the most wonderful desserts like tarte au sucre and tarte aux raisins.

Back then, the countryside was blanketed with farmers' fields, as many people lived by farming. Donald's dad also had a job on the side, working in a garage to earn some money to buy the things they couldn't make at home. But it was mostly subsistence farming. They were self-sufficient, following the seasons, planting in the spring, harvesting in the summer, slaughtering in the fall and salting the meat to make it through the long winter.

The day I arrived in Acadieville, the harvest was drawing to a close. A warm spell had moved into the area, with the forecast calling for a few more days of balmy weather. It was early November, and most of the vegetables had been picked; however, there were still some cabbages to be collected, carrots to be dug and other chores to take care of before the snow. We took the truck to the back acreage to see how Yvon, a neighbour who works for Donald, was doing with the ploughing. The field he was tilling was set deep in the forest—we had to drive off the main road, down a bumpy dirt lane, first past some fields and then through the woods to get there. When the first Acadian settlers moved into the area, the Crown was giving away land in 100-acre plots on the condition that the newcomers clear fifteen acres of each parcel for farming, Donald explained. The fields they opened were the flattest, easiest patches of land to clear of trees and underbrush and not necessarily near the road. This means that today, many of Donald's fields—he works about four hundred acres spread over twenty farms so he can rotate his crops to maintain the health of the soil—are virtually hidden from sight, tucked away behind forests and rivers.

Even if you knew where to look, not all of this agricultural land remains. Much of the fields the Acadians cleared for food production have since grown over. As we made our way across the countryside in Donald's truck, he pointed to forests that were farms when he was a child. Most of the farmers of his youth have gone out of business and let the land go fallow. The family farm is just about an anachronism in these parts. In fact, farmers across the Maritimes aren't doing well. Signs of economic decay are all around: a rusted old school bus lies abandoned in someone's yard, the charred shadow of a burned-down barn casts a pall over one farm, and Acadieville's elementary school no longer has enough pupils to keep its doors open, a bad omen for the future. Farms have been either hard to sell—a neighbour of Donald and Viola's passed away, leaving his house to a distant relation who, after he couldn't sell it to anyone else, ended up gifting the property to the couple for one dollar as thanks for their help through the years—or desirable only to buyers who intend to strip the topsoil and sell it for potting, or build a big house and retire, not farm. That's why Donald and the folks at the Really Local knew that if they were going to keep their communities vital, they needed to find a way to preserve the family farm.

·

When I think of the family farm, I conjure up a picture of a house and barn set against the backdrop of rows of crops and some cows, maybe a horse or some goats or sheep, grazing in a field; a farm tended by a family. The family farm in Canada is a cultural icon, an archetype of life in this country that has inspired ideals of nationhood. And it is on this kind of farm that we often presume our food is grown. Assumptions about what characterizes this institution run along these lines: agriculture as practised by a family on a piece of land that they own. This family is independent and entrepreneurial and can enjoy the fruits of its own labour. Farming for them is a way of life. Although this kind of farming was common fifty years ago, it's disappearing quickly in the twenty-first century—some would say that the family farm doesn't even exist anymore. Certainly when you look at the New Brunswick countryside around Acadieville, it would be easy to conclude that the family farm is going the way of the passenger pigeon.

One of the people who argues the family farm in Canada is now extinct is Tony Fuller, a professor with the School of Environmental Design and Rural Development at the University of Guelph. Fuller, who is originally from Blackpool, England, has spent his career studying farming and rural life in Canada. Over his lifetime, he has witnessed the changes first-hand. Back in 1969, on the first day of his Agriculture Geography group at Guelph, he asked if anyone in the class could show him around the countryside and introduce him to real farming in Canada. Every weekend, one of the students took him out, and in this way, Fuller got to know how people farmed back then. Comparing what he saw on these trips to what he sees these days, he argues that independence, one of the fundamental qualities people have always valued about farming, has eroded. That's why he says the family farm doesn't exist the way it used to.

Today there are two extremes in agriculture, he posits. On one end of the spectrum are small operations. "When you drive by, for all intents and purposes, it looks like it's a family farm. But when you examine the relationship with farming, it's small. If they depended on the farm, they'd go bankrupt," he said. These smaller farms often carry high debt loads, and the family works off the farm to pay the bills. "Most family farms are owned by the bank," Fuller said. "The returns from agriculture on a small scale are so small, it wouldn't allow them to furnish their debt, even a modest debt, given the price of land and the cost of inputs." At the other end of the spectrum are the large agribusiness operations where farmers are contracted to cultivate thousands of acres of land or raise tens of thousands of hogs or chickens for a specific company. "They may look like a family farm—there is a man and a woman and a farm—but really they are working for McCain or Cargill," said Fuller. Even though, on paper, these large operations are worth millions of dollars—the barns, the pedigree of the livestock, the machinery—the farmers carry such enormous debt and the profit margins are so small on their product that at the end of the day, they are in a similar position to the small farmer. That is, they are not making much of a living on the farm.

"The biggest change is the gradual loss of relative independence that was the chief marker of the family farm," said Fuller. "It used to be that the farmer woke up every day and said, I think I'll plough that field or walk that cow from here to there. But the contract farmers know exactly what they are going to do every day because they have to feed the pigs in time for the truck to arrive to take them away. This isn't the kind of farming you write poetry or paint pictures about."

In Canada, there used to be many family farms. In 1951, there were 600,000 family farms across Canada. According to Statistics Canada data, today there are almost 230,000. Changes on the family farm have been precipitated by advances in technology and science as well as by government policies intended to modernize agriculture. A quick over-view of the history of farming since the Second World War traces the causes of what's happened.

In the 1950s, government programs encouraged farmers to get bigger, buy more land and increase production—a growth that was facilitated by the tractor. (In the next chapter, I'll delve more deeply into how the tractor changed farming.) Throughout the next decade, bigger was seen as better. The family farm was considered to be inefficient and antiquated.

Government told farmers to adapt to the new consolidated reality of farming or to get out of the business. In 1962, the federal government passed the Agriculture and Rural Development Act to consolidate farms into ever bigger units of production. The slogan of the day was "people to jobs," and farmers were encouraged to leave the farm for town. The land they left behind was bought or leased by the Ministry of Lands and Forests for reforestation. Those who stayed on the land were encouraged to specialize in, say, hog farming or corn cropping, and then practise on a large scale, employing technology and capital.

By the 1970s the future of farming in North America looked great. International stores of wheat and rice were extremely low, which meant grain prices shot up. There was talk of worldwide food shortages—despite the advances of the Green Revolution, it was feared that the world might not be able to feed its growing population. Farmers in North America seized the opportunity and started to produce more and more food. Farms increased in size, and both the government and the banks were happy to facilitate this expansion by lending money. With low interest rates and high inflation, it made economic sense to bulk up on acreage by borrowing the money against the rising value of farmland they already owned to further increase production. There was the pervasive belief that farming would become ever more profitable as the numbers of mouths to feed grew exponentially around the world.

But the golden days never do last as long as we think they will. At the end of the 1970s, a combination of global trends changed everything. North American farms were producing more food than the rest of the world wanted to buy. The price of oil was rising, as were interest rates. Suddenly farmers had a cash flow problem because they couldn't make enough money to service the debts they had incurred expanding their farms.

The Farm Crisis began in the early 1980s. It was a brutal time for farmers in Canada. In 1983 in Ontario alone 488 farmers went bankrupt. The next year it was 551. These numbers don't include the farms that were foreclosed by the bank or the families who quit before they lost everything. And the farmers were angry. In Ontario, a group of men in Grey County formed Farm Gate Defence to forcibly stop the banks from taking over their friends' farms. In April of 1982, a group of 150 farmers from Grey and Bruce counties, frustrated by the spiralling situation on the farm, drove into Toronto in the middle of the night and blockaded the Ontario Food Terminal in an attempt to cut off the city's food supply.

What was happening on the farm was so dramatic that it made headlines across the country. But the media attention didn't change much, and soon the flame of the farm crisis died down, disappearing from the public eye. But the core issues never went away. Farming in Canada has never recovered. According to the National Farmers Union, a farm crisis persists in Canada. Farmers today earn less than they did in the desperate times of the Great Depression. The union predicts that this will drive people off the farm and by 2025, we'll be left with half of the farmers there are now.[4]

What happened to farming in Canada through the decades after the Second World War not only affected the size and scale of farms but fundamentally changed our perception of agriculture. The disappearance of the family farm is directly related to the shift in the way we understand how food is produced. Whereas the family farm used to be a way of life and an income for a family, today farming is a business. Farmers are referred to as "producers"; the foods they produce are "commodities." They capitalize their operations and technologize, striving for greater efficiencies. Most of our food is produced on large farms, the agribusiness operations, rather than on the small farms, so these big farms are the first link in the industrial food chain. It was this shift in farming that helped to bring us industrial food as we know it today.

The way our society views food—as a commodity not unlike a toaster or a sweater—is a reflection of the kind of food we eat. It's no wonder our supermarkets and even drugstores are packed with processed foods, concocted of high-fructose corn syrup (such as pop, cookies and pre-made pasta sauce), factory-farmed beef, pork and poultry (boxes of frozen burgers, bacon, chicken fingers), and modified milk ingredients (processed cheese, diet yogurt, pellet-shaped ice cream you eat with your fingers). If this kind of food is a product of the industrial food chain, then imagine what would happen to the food we eat if we were to change the supply chain that begins on the farm.

What's happening on the farm is relevant to those of us who want to build a new and sustainable foodshed for Canadian society. To create a local food system, we must redefine the farm. We must transform it into the kind of institution that produces the kind of food we want to eat. This is happening all across Canada. And in Acadieville, it's a real success.

· · ·

Once upon a time, farmers made a decent living in New Brunswick. Around Acadieville in the 1960s, in an area encompassing towns such as Rogersville, St. Louis and Richibouctou, there were several dozen vegetable growers. They cultivated more than a thousand acres of produce, the majority of it destined for the McCain processing plant a few hundred kilometres to the west, in Florenceville. In the mid-twentieth century, potatoes dominated—McCain started freezing and selling french fries in 1957 and relied on local growers for a steady supply of potatoes. But after farmers started to grow Brussels sprouts in the 1950s, this popular brassica quickly took over and remained a pillar of the local economy for the next three decades. During this period, there were six hundred acres of the thick green stalks growing out of the southeastern New Brunswick soil. The legacy of their popularity is apparent to this day on the menu at one of Rogersville's three restaurants, Chez Doris, where Brussels sprouts and cheese sauce is offered as a regular side dish. Donald's father-in-law was one of the farmers who relied on this vegetable and cultivated more than sixty acres.

Not only did Brussels sprouts support the farmers, but they contributed to other economic activity as well. To operate their farms, people needed to buy equipment, so dealerships existed to supply the latest machinery such as tractors and tillers, and gas stations sold the diesel to fuel them. Then there were jobs for pickers and farmhands. As well, Brussels sprouts grow on big, thick stalks from which the small cabbage-like sprouts are cut. The foliage that is left behind after the vegetables are harvested was used to feed the local beef cattle or was ploughed back into the ground as organic fertilizer. All this spinoff kept the community afloat.

Then one day globalization came to town. In the early 1980s McCain started to buy Brussels sprouts grown elsewhere. The New Brunswick crops, plus their freight costs, were not the lowest priced. In 1986, the processing plant shut down (McCain stopped producing frozen Brussels sprouts entirely in Canada in 1992). The closing was bad news for the farmers, since they'd been selling to McCain for decades and they knew of no other market for their produce. At first, they tried to survive by selling the vegetables to the fresh market, but six hundred acres of fresh Brussels sprouts are not exactly easy to move.

Around the same time, Donald was just getting into Brussels sprouts—when the plant closed, he'd been in the business two years. Like his neighbours, he was hit hard. So the next year, he planted cauliflower and cabbage and turned to the grocery market, along with many of the other farmers who'd been shut out. But this was no easy fix either. Selling directly to the grocery stores proved to be extremely difficult. The farmers had to incur a whole new set of costs: it was their responsibility to deliver their produce to the warehouse, something they hadn't done when the McCain truck picked up their vegetables. This meant buying new trucks, servicing them and paying for the fuel to drive the hundred kilometres to the stores. And they had to pay the grocery companies a registration fee to be allowed to sell to them in the first place—this money came right off their cheques.

Some farmers, hoping to secure some income, signed contracts with these large companies to grow an agreed-upon number of acres of a desired vegetable, like corn or broccoli, that would be distributed in the chain stores. However, often when it was time to harvest, the company would back out of the contract at the last minute, explained Patrice Finnigan, Donald's brother-in-law, a greenhouse grower who is a founding member of the co-op.[5] Patrice is also known as Mr. Tomato for the thousands of tomatoes he grows every year in his Rogersville greenhouses.

My visit to Rogersville to learn about the Really Local Harvest Co-op began with a lunch with Donald and Patrice at Chez Doris, where, in addition to Brussels sprouts in a cheese sauce, they serve Donald's potatoes. To understand why the co-op has been important for the farmers, they said that I had to first understand how difficult it was to make any money farming in their area in the days when they relied on supermarkets to buy their vegetables.

"You could call up the warehouse and say we've got 100 boxes of broccoli. Do you want them?" said Donald. "And they'd say, no, we're backed up. I just got a shipment of broccoli from California."

Once, Patrice's tomatoes got crushed in the grocer's truck and they refused to pay him for the fruit until he threatened them with a lawsuit.

"How many did we lose?" Patrice asked Donald.

"We lost everybody," said Donald.

"The same week we have our potatoes coming out they put imported potatoes on for half price. They are killing us little by little," said Patrice. "They've created a system where we can't fit anymore."

The farmers hit rock bottom around the summer of 1997. The grocery warehouses in New Brunswick where they had been reluctantly selling their product shut down, leaving even fewer buyers. No one knew what to do. Donald said the dire state of the situation was summed up best by what was happening on the local U-pick strawberry farms. The six farms, all growing the berries for the same market, became embroiled in a deep price war. The signs at the side of the road that lured pickers were testimony to just how bad it was: the original low price of 75 cents a pound was struck out. Beside it was a big 69 cents with an X through it, leaving the price at 50 cents a pound. These prices were so low that they didn't even cover the cost of producing the berries. The farmers were selling the strawberries—and just about everything else—for less than the cost of production.

"We were all doing our own thing on our own farms and we hoped the guy next door would kick the bucket before we did," said Patrice.

"We thought if the neighbour lost his shirt, we would do better," said Donald. "But even though we were losing our neighbours, we weren't doing any better."

Then, a group of six farmers that included Patrice got together and realized that the only way to save the family farm was to sell directly to the consumer. They figured that cutting out the middle man would be the first step to making more money. Already some of these farmers were selling to the public at the farm gate, and some had farm stands and only needed to trade between themselves to offer a diverse selection to their customers. So Patrice sold Donald's potatoes, someone else's corn and another farmer's apples. Other members of the group opened stalls too, and sales started to take off.

By 2000, the group had officially registered as a co-operative. Today they have thirty farms spread over three counties in southeastern New Brunswick. Their mandate is to assist members in increasing their profits while selling an ecologically sustainable product at a reasonable price. The co-operative is run by a board of directors, elected from the general membership. Members meet at least four times a year, usually gathering at each other's farms, to make decisions collectively about marketing strategies and the day-to-day running of the co-op. They close the door and no one leaves until they gain a consensus of sorts—they know that not everybody will agree with the group's every decision, but they believe that each farmer must be comfortable living with its repercussions. When the co-op is faced with a serious issue, members volunteer for a working group to study the matter and write up a list of pros and cons. Then a vote is held. Once a year, the farmers all gather for a general meeting, which often turns into a big picnic with their families. Some farmers have left the group over the years and new people do join. But by maintaining the collective decision making and adhering to the co-op's founding philosophy of fairness and sustainability, Donald said they ensure that everybody works together towards the same goal.

It was in this way that they decided the best way to help the customer to see the value in buying their local produce instead of imported food at the supermarket was to highlight the ways their produce was different. So they created their own brand, which they called Eco-Logik, and designed a logo so consumers could easily identify local produce and know at a glance that it was grown in a sustainable way. To earn the right to sell under the Eco-Logik brand, farmers must adhere to provincial and federal agricultural regulations, test their irrigation water for pathogens like *E. coli* and keep up-to-date financial records. Even though the majority of farms aren't organic, they must agree to an alternative weed and pest control system to reduce the amount of chemicals they use. Not only is this better for the land, explained Donald, but it reduces the costs of production, thus pushing up profits.

Once the farmers understood the links between expenses and profits—thinking like business people for the first time in their careers—they started to calculate the costs of production before setting their price. As a member of the co-op, you have to sign a contract pledging not to sell your produce at a loss. When the strawberry growers realized that they would have to double the U-pick price to make a profit, they shook their heads in disbelief.

However, through the years the price has more than doubled, sales are good, and the growers are making real profits. After an adjustment period, consumers realized that they were paying for a higher-quality and better-tasting berry. Local strawberries were worth the extra cost.

•

What the Really Local Harvest Co-op is building in New Brunswick is what Larry Yee, University of California advisor emeritus and co-founder of the Association of Family Farms in California, calls "value-based value chains," an academic expression to describe a food system that is founded on more than profit making. His organization was created to save the disappearing family farm because Yee and his colleagues believe this kind of agriculture has an important role in the food chain. They call it agriculture of the middle, the middle being neither the farms that have nominal output nor large industrial operations but rather the mid-sized family farm that grows a good amount of food such as the farms in the Really Local Harvest Co-op. "It's typically the farm that we all idyllically have in our mind's eye. We think of that red barn with the silo and the verdant fields, the farmhouse. And we think about the farmer being in charge of the operation," explained Yee. "We've tried putting numbers around it. We're probably talking a gross revenue of somewhere between $50,000 and $1 million." It's these farms that they want to preserve because they tend to grow the food that people are looking for when they want to eat locally. These farms are the link in the food chain that is best suited to a sustainable local foodshed.

According to Yee, the reason these types of farms work well in a local food economy is that they can easily adapt to a new food chain built on an entirely different set of values than the ones favoured by our current system. "The type of food system we've created, it's been developed for the larger scale, the more efficient," he said. "In a different type of food system, one we imagine to be more balanced and healthy, you are going to be deriving value not necessarily from efficiencies of scale but from the differentiation of production. You are producing a different food product that has qualities people are looking for." These qualities, which are not necessarily reflected by price, include being grown from heirloom seed stock or without chemicals, being humanely raised or freshly picked or being produced on a farm the customer is able to visit.

For this kind of system to function, every link in the supply chain must be treated equitably, from the farmer all the way to the consumer. Farmers are able to set their prices and cover their costs of production while consumers gain knowledge about what they are buying. Relationships are cultivated on trust and people co-operate rather than compete with each other, just as in the Really Local Harvest Co-op. "The chain actually acts as a bridge from producer to consumer," said Yee. "Market signals go back and forth. People say, this is what kind of food we are looking for. Farmers are saying, this is my food and this is how it's grown."

It's not only in New Brunswick where people are creating these alternative food chains that attach worth to qualities other than money. Community-supported agriculture, also known as a CSA, is an arrangement whereby people purchase shares in a farmer's crops in exchange for a box of produce each week—is one way of linking farmers directly to their customers—and is also one of the qualities Yee cites. CSAs are rising in popularity. In 1990, there were sixty in North America. Today there are more than seventeen hundred, and the Rodale Institute, a Pennsylvania-based agricultural think tank, predicts this number is likely to quadruple over the next few years. An indication of the CSA's imminent shift from the cultural fringes to the mainstream is a billboard at the side of Highway 404 that heads north from Toronto, advertising a local farm's CSA.

An integral part of every CSA is Yee's value-based value chain. And the values CSAs represent are an important part of a local food system in Canada.

■   ■   ■

When Donald told me about the Gagnon family, one of the members of the co-op, I immediately wanted to meet them. Even though their farm is tucked away down the back roads and hard to find, I knew I must talk to them before I left New Brunswick. The story of their family farm follows the larger narrative of what has happened to agriculture over the last few decades, but then takes a U-turn and becomes an example of a prospering local and sustainable food system with the same values Yee celebrates. So, despite harsh weather, Donald and I climbed into his truck and headed off to their place.

The Gagnon family farm is down a dirt road, pot-holed by rain and heavy machinery. It's built on a small incline overlooking a forest. The bush is dense and, save for the evergreens, the vista when I was there was mostly grey. The leaves had fallen from the trees and the rain was coming down hard. Jean-Pierre and his dad, Paul, were working in the barn with a crew of labourers. They were building a new wing, four large pens for their mama sows, which had grown too big and too numerous for the old place. Just like a number of the other farmers in the co-op, they were in expansion mode. Jean-Pierre is thirty-two years old and taller than his dad, who hunched in a yellow rain slicker and baseball cap. Jean-Pierre seemed older than his years, maybe because he spoke softly and knowingly, with the wisdom of someone who has seen a lot. Like his dad, he is a slender man, lean from the hard work that's required of them on the farm where they keep hogs, lambs, chickens and beef cattle. They raise this livestock mostly on the hay and grains they grow themselves, and, in their farm abattoir, they prepare the meats to sell directly to their customers.

Jean-Pierre was two when his parents purchased the farm in 1979, and the family has been in and out of the business ever since. While today they are one of the big-time success stories of the Really Local Harvest Co-op, the recent good years are still outnumbered by the bad. Growing up on the farm, Jean-Pierre watched his parents struggle to keep at what they wanted to do. They ran a sow maternity barn, raising baby pigs to sell to commercial hog operations. The problem was, no matter what they did on the farm, they could never seem to turn a profit. Then in 1982 things worsened. Interest rates spiked to more than 20 percent, the price of pork fell, and when the family failed to make the payments on their mortgage, the Farm Credit Office foreclosed on the farm. Three years earlier, the Farm Credit Office had loaned them the money to buy the farm and build the hog barn, but that summer they took control of the property and put it up for auction.

In an interesting turn of events, Jean-Pierre's dad was able to bid in the auction and buy the place back. But they didn't return to farming. They left the barns empty and worked off-farm—his dad had an income-tax and bookkeeping business in a nearby town and his mother was a nurse. In 1991, they bought some pigs, but after two years they quit the pork business again because there still wasn't any money in it.

When it came time for Jean-Pierre to decide what he wanted to do with his life after he finished school, he looked west to Alberta's booming oil economy. "I just saw no future in farming," he told me. "I watched my father work one to two extra jobs constantly to support his true passion, which was farming. It didn't seem like a credible business to get into. The love was there—I grew up watching my dad do the things he loved. It just wasn't viable." But life in Alberta wasn't like life in New Brunswick, and Jean-Pierre wanted to settle down. Even though he was working hard and making good money in construction—money his parents had never seen in their lifetimes—he didn't feel satisfied. When he met his wife, Sherry, in Calgary and they had a baby girl, all the time he spent at work rather than at home felt like too steep a trade-off for economic security. Jean-Pierre called his dad and told him that he was coming back to New Brunswick. He didn't know what he was going to do, but the three of them would be staying on the farm until they figured it out. To celebrate his son's return, Paul bought twenty sheep, twenty pigs and sixty chickens, unwittingly sowing the seeds of his son's future.

It was the beginning of August 2002 when Jean-Pierre and his young family returned from Alberta. He didn't feel the push to find work right away because the family had some money saved and there was a second house on his parents' property where they could stay. A few weeks later, they threw a party for their friends. When the fifth person that night asked him what he'd be doing now that he was back in New Brunswick, he mused that he was going into farming. "I jokingly said I have some pork for sale. People jumped at it. They remembered the quality of the meat they used to get from our farm and they wanted to buy some." Jean-Pierre and his dad ended up selling their first quarter of pork that night. "It just flew from there," he said. Very quickly Jean-Pierre learned that he could earn a living selling meat directly to the consumer.

Their first day at the Moncton Farmers' Market was Thanksgiving weekend. They went with two sides of pork and twenty-five chickens and were sold out by 9:30 a.m. Today, the Gagnon operation is fully functional. What was once a money-losing business now employs seven people, plus Jean-Pierre and his dad; his sister Natalie, who had left the farm for work in Ottawa, has returned to New Brunswick to work part-time at the farmers' markets, a busy job since the Gagnons are the only farm in the Really Local Harvest Co-op that provides meat.

The barns on the Gagnon farm reminded me of the farms in my children's story books. There is a pastoral, almost olden-days quality about them. Even though it was cold outside, the air inside was warm, with a fresh, earthy smell. The pigs rushed to the side of the pen, wagging their tails and sticking their noses and hoofs and whatever else they could through the slats in a furious attempt to find out who I was. In the next room, the chickens cooed and slowly moved away from us, making their way towards the big windows that cast light inside. They had spent the summer and most of the fall outdoors and were only just starting to get used to their new home.

The Gagnons raise their animals like people did before industrial agriculture. "We went back fifty years and took what they had then and brought it back for today," Jean-Pierre explained. All the livestock are grass-fed. In the fields, they grow the timothy and clover that they hay for the pigs. These animals spend the summers in a veranda-style area of the barn where they are exposed to the fresh air yet shaded from the sun; because of their fair skin, they can't stay in the fields for the summer. The cows and sheep, however, pasture in the warm months of the year, and the laying hens stay out as long as the weather permits, feeding on grass, supplemented with corn and grains. The Gagnons treat the animals with respect—the pigs are each allotted about ten square feet that is covered with straw bedding. (Industrial farms keep their animals cheek-by-jowl in concrete pens.) Also, they don't give their animals any stimulants, hormones, medicines or antibiotics. In 2005, Jean-Pierre worked with the Really Local Harvest Co-op and three agronomists from the province to incorporate their methods into the co-op's standards so that any future members would have to raise their animals in the same way.

Across the rainy yard, the sheep jumped up to rest their hoofs on the fence, bleated, and tried to get a better look at what was going on. Jean-Pierre headed back to work. I left, excited at having seen the new family farm well and thriving in New Brunswick.

·

The Dieppe Farmers' Market is located on a typical suburban streetscape just outside Moncton. Not far away, down the wide avenue jammed with cars and SUVs, are Walmart, Sobey's, the Atlantic Co-op—the big-name chains where people have grown used to shopping for groceries. But on Saturday mornings, the market is the place where they prefer to come. Every week, about seven thousand people walk into this barn-like modern structure jammed with kiosks selling Jean-Pierre's meats, Patrice's tomatoes and Donald's potatoes as well as local cheeses, vegetables, cranberries—everything the co-op members produce. The market is the crowning glory of the Really Local Harvest Co-op. They founded it in 2005 in co-operation with the City of Dieppe, and have since turned it into one of the most successful farmers' markets in the region. "People don't go to church anymore," said Donald. "But on Saturday mornings, now they are going to the market. What happened in church—the gossip, the shaking of hands—it's happening at the market."

As profitable as the network of farm-gate stalls has been for the members of the Really Local, the co-op's prosperity is inextricably linked to the Dieppe market. Before it opened, people in Dieppe felt the city lacked a centre, that there was nothing to root the community. They decided a farmers' market was what their town needed to ground it, make it something special. Someone had heard about the Really Local, and officials approached the co-op to see if they were interested in working together on some sort of plan. The farmers liked the idea, and within a year, funding was secured, a building was leased and the farmers were running their own market. The appetite for local food in the region was enormous: on opening day, ten thousand people came to see what the farmers were offering.

On an average Saturday morning, it's hard to even move around the place, it gets so busy. In 2008, the market grossed more than $4 million. People are drawn to the food, flocking to the stands selling fiddleheads and rhubarb in the spring and tomatoes, zucchini and bunched carrots in the summer, cranberries and root vegetables in the fall. One organic vegetable farmer is regularly sold out before noon. The farmers' market has given the co-op's members a real boost. And the success has been noted by farmers around the globe. Farmers' organizations from Australia and Burkino Faso have sent representatives to New Brunswick to learn from the Really Local and witness what they've accomplished.

Donald Daigle no longer runs the co-op, having stepped down after eight years. He is now a bit of a celebrity on the farm circuit. He spends time on the road, talking to groups across the country, seeing parts of

Canada he had never visited before. When he's home, people call him up to ask his opinion about all sorts of topics related to agriculture. But for Donald, one of the most profound signs of the co-op's success is the interest the next generation shows in taking over the farm now that they see they can make a living there. When Donald was young, farming was his dream. But when his eldest son, Jereme, turned nineteen and told his dad he wanted to work on the farm, Donald discouraged him. "I said, no, you are too young. Go out and see the world. Go out and see things. You will always wonder what's out there if you don't go and see for yourself."

Jereme went out to Alberta to work, but soon enough he came home. They're looking into cranberry farms now. Donald feels the time is right for his son to start farming. In the same way that the Really Local changed agriculture in New Brunswick, the next generation of farmers like Donald's son will transform the way we farm in Canada and help to build a local food system here.

CHAPTER TWO

WHO'S NEXT?

Nova Scotia's Next Generation of Farmers

"Had I known then what we would go through, I wouldn't have done it," said Greg Gerrits, a thirty-eight-year-old vegetable farmer in the Annapolis Valley in Nova Scotia. We were standing in his sloping carrot field minutes after dozens of tubs of the bright orange root crop were pulled from the ground. "Had I known then what we would go through, I wouldn't have done it," he repeated, meaning had he known how difficult it would have been to take over his father's farm at the outset, he would have chosen a career other than farming. Greg repeated this statement to me at least two times during my visit, first standing in the fields amid the peppery smell of the freshly harvested carrots and then later at the dining-room table, after lunch, with his wife, Suzanne, sitting to his left nodding sombrely.

It has been a difficult struggle for them to take over the family farm and start their own vegetable business. While other farm kids are often given their parents' property (which generally means assuming their parents' debt load, so no free ride), this was not the case for Greg. His family is originally from Holland and, Greg said, in his culture you don't inherit, you *earn* your parents' property through hard labour. So Greg paid for his swath of Nova Scotian farmland with, literally, blood (when you harvest broccoli you use a knife and someone always ends up with a cut), sweat (in the summer it gets so hot, first your shirt sticks to your back and then every bit of dust clings to your skin) and tears (there were occasions when the frustration got so fierce that all there was left to do was cry).

The Gerritses' farm is at the eastern end of the Annapolis Valley, where the soil and the climate are good. The early springs that touch the area afford a mid-June harvest, and a mild fall hangs around well into November, allowing for carrots, parsley, broccoli, even lettuce to be picked after Halloween. Farmers have been attracted here for centuries. And it's beautiful countryside too. The hilly land tapers into the Bay of Fundy to the east and is interspersed with dykes of brick-red sand that fill and empty along with the tides. When I visited, it was fall and the landscape was a mottled green. The farmhouses appeared to be huddling near the edge of the roads, the fields stretching out around them. Every few dozen kilometres or so I passed another old church with a small graveyard, the trees around the tombstones bare of leaves. A handwritten sign outside one of these many churches offered an open invitation: "Card Party, 7:30 Tuesdays." I got the sense of an ageing population.

At Elmridge Farm they were preparing the carrots for winter storage. Two men from Jamaica, whom Greg and Suzanne had hired through the foreign workers program, helped Greg to load bins of carrots onto a wooden contraption resting on a front-end loader that Greg had built himself.[6] They'd just perfected their use of the carrot harvester, and Greg was pleased with the 100 tubs they'd filled in only half an hour. The machine was an old one he'd bought for $3,000 (new ones cost more than $40,000) and fixed himself. To be a farmer, "you've got to know how to tinker," he said. When the workers finished filling the bins with carrots, they began moving them to an outbuilding near the barn, where they would wash them and then put them in cold storage.

After the workers had driven off, Greg stood in the field and perused the crops visible from the top of the hill. He wore a navy blue coverall over his long and wiry frame. His hair was short and quite grey for someone his age. He bent down to pick a carrot from a nearby bin, rubbed a bit of the sandy earth off on his pant leg, and absentmindedly took a bite. He stared at the south-facing slope, down from where we stood, at the blue hue of leeks seen at a distance, as well as spinach, lettuce and kale. "It's good vegetable land. It's the earliest place this side of Quebec. That's our advantage," he said. The orientation of his fields to the south means he can get his produce to an early market. Greg also works hard to build the fertility of his fields with cover crops and manure, so they can continue to provide him with the yields he's grown accustomed to. It was his dad who cleared the carrot field when Greg was a teenager, and he's witnessed the earth here turn from granular, almost sandy, to rich soil. He leaned down to pick up a handful of it to show me. It's a deep red colour, what he called a sand hump deposited by glaciers, but now with the dark, earthy quality of organic matter.

As he talked, I watched a blue jay fly over our heads on its way to the white spruce at the edge of the field. The air was soft and damp on my cheek. Standing there, I understood immediately why Greg was pulled back to the land where he grew up. He was the only one of five siblings interested in taking over the farm. His brother, now a computer programmer, had allergies that ruled out farming as an occupation and his three sisters all went to university to study in non-agricultural fields. Greg was the only one who, as a child, worked steadily in the barn. "When did I join my dad on the farm?" he asked. "When I was four years old. When I was in high school, I was working forty hours a week while going to school full-time." Working on the farm was something he never questioned. He liked the work—he still does—and got to do all sorts of things his friends couldn't, like drive a tractor. Then he went to agricultural college in Truro, where he studied agronomy. After he finished his degree, he returned home with the goal of buying the farm from his dad, just like his father had done a generation before. When he married Suzanne a few years later, their plan was to buy the place from his parents and build a vegetable business. They had two kids, Gillian and later James. Finally, in 2003, a full decade after Greg returned to the farm, they officially bought the property.

The big question was, could they make a go of farming? At a time when more farmers were leaving the profession than joining, would they ever make the money they needed to support their family?

.

From the minute I arrived at Elmridge Farm, I was nagged by some statistics. According to the numbers, Greg (twenty-three when he started farming in 1993) and Suzanne don't actually exist. The average age of farmers in Canada is fifty-two, according to the 2006 census. That rose from an average of forty-nine years in 2001, which indicates that not many new farmers like Greg have joined the ranks this century. In that same period, *twenty thousand* Canadian farmers left the profession. And the farmers who quit are often the young ones, abandoning ship before they sink into indebtedness.

If the average age of farmers is climbing, and the younger ones are leaving in droves, I wonder who is going to grow our food. In the next ten years, when it's time for these fifty-odd-year-old farmers to retire, who is going to go out into the fields? Today, the demand for locally grown food might be on a steep rise, with people in cities clamouring for free-run eggs and heirloom vegetables tenderly raised by farmers in neighbouring rural areas, but are there enough farmers left to meet this demand tomorrow? Is it already too late to have discovered the pleasures—and environmental benefits—of local eating?

The extremes of this situation are epitomized for me every time I visit the St. Lawrence Market in downtown Toronto. There is only one farm stand that sells eggs on Saturday mornings. Theirs are free-run, grain-fed and antibiotic-free eggs, and there is always a crowd of people at their table, jostling to be first in line, with handfuls of toonies and loonies. If you arrive late, you likely won't find the selection that's available earlier in the day. An elderly farmer and his wife used to stand behind the table counting the change in the palms of their hands, reaching as if in slow motion for another carton. But the man passed away in the fall of 2009. His wife continues to come to market, some younger women helping her with the eggs, but I've found myself standing there watching her contend with the throng, my heart panging away. In due course, she too won't be coming to the market anymore. So where are all us keen downtown city folk going to get our farm-fresh eggs if there's no one to replace the farmers when they go?

Another chapter in the story of the disappearing family farm in Canada is the question of farm succession. Most of the farm kids that Greg grew up with haven't, on the whole, taken over their parents' farms as he has, and this partly explains why there are fewer and fewer farms in Canada. The number of farms in this country peaked in 1941, with 732,832 operations. More than sixty years later, this number has dropped by almost 70 percent. In the Maritimes, where Greg Gerrits farms, the numbers fell off even more precipitously, with only 15 percent of the region's farms left in operation by the mid-1980s. The children of farmers have left their family's profession at a rapid rate because farm kids haven't wanted to farm as generations did before them. When you grow up seeing your parents work really hard for little financial reward, following their example is not an appealing career choice. And judging from what Greg told me, they are not wrong.

When I asked him why more young people weren't farming like him and Suzanne, he chuckled. The morning's carrot harvest had gone well, and we'd come in for lunch. Suzanne had made soup from their vegetables—broccoli, kale, carrots, onions—and we each microwaved a bowl to eat with some olive bread she had picked up at the local bakery. (She laughed that all this interest in local food was changing her shopping habits too and she had wanted to try this new bread that was baked nearby.) After we finished eating, when it was time to go back to the fields—Greg needed to bury irrigation pipe before the snow arrived—he lingered at the dining-room table. I made to get up, but then realized he was not going anywhere just yet; he was enjoying these few moments away from the farm work that made up his days. In the ten years they'd been farming, it wasn't often that either of them had the chance to sit down during the day.

There is only hard work on the farm, and Greg and Suzanne spend six and a half days a week, fifty-two weeks of the year doing it. Even though Greg believes you must take Sunday off, there is always something to take care of then. On an average day in the summer, it is up with the first light, well before six, so Greg can eat and glance at the paper before he heads out to meet the crew. At around seven, they start filling orders, planting, harvesting, weeding, seeding, hoeing, whatever has to be done that day. It's steady work till about six o'clock, when it's time for supper. But if there's a farmers' market the next day, then work reaches a frenetic pace in the evening and often goes into the night. Everybody must pitch in to pick and clean the produce in time to take it to town. Then it's up in the wee hours, around two, to pack the truck and drive to market; the kids, now nine and seven, come too.

"Everyone else has fun with their kids on Saturday. We don't get to go camping or take family vacations—even to go away for the day," said Suzanne, who, after handling the market in Halifax on Saturday still doesn't get a break since she must prepare the payroll for their thirty employees before Monday. In the summer, they each work about eighty-five hours a week, which drops to fifty-five hours in the winter when the bookkeeping, preparing seeds and general planning takes place.

If you calculated the money Greg and Suzanne make per hour, it would be shockingly little. When they first started on the farm, Greg's tax return showed $14,500 a year in income. From that, they paid $500 a month in rent to his parents and then $2,500 to the taxman. That left them with $6,000 to take care of their family of four for the year. In 2002, "it got to the point where I was wearing boots with my feet hanging out," remembered Greg.

The problem isn't the amount of work but rather the amount of money they are paid for the food they grow. Then there have been the problems of selling to the wholesaler who supplies the supermarket chains nearby. For four years, Greg grew broccoli for the wholesaler. Even though he'd sign a contract with them in the spring, promising to supply them with produce at harvest, it didn't work out as they'd expected. One Friday evening, Greg trucked $5,000 worth of broccoli to the wholesaler's cooler that the company was planning to ship on Monday morning. But the cooler broke down on the weekend, the broccoli spoiled, and the wholesaler wouldn't pay for the vegetables they could no longer sell. Greg and Suzanne took the loss.

Things have changed since the day Greg's granddad arrived in Canada from the Netherlands in 1953, when you could expect to raise a family and live a good life on the farm. This is because a patchwork of influences were at play in the years between the Second World War and the turn of the century that dramatically changed rural life in Canada. In addition to debt and the farm crisis, technological change has transformed the farm. And one of the biggest changes came when farmers replaced their horses with the tractor.

·

The Massey Ferguson, the John Deere—these tractors have been making their way up and down the corn rows for decades, though today in North America, tractors are just as likely to carry the brand name Kubota or Mahindra, manufactured in Japan and India respectively, two countries making inroads into the North American tractor market. These are expensive machines. An entry-level model, the equivalent of a compact car, costs about $80,000. An SUV-level tractor would set you back about $150,000. Then you would need to pay for diesel and equipment and repairs. Despite the high cost, tractors have been the single most transformative tool on the farm since the mid-century, when they replaced horse-power and human sweat. The tractor can plough your field, plant it, spray it, cut and crimp the hay you grow in it, then rake it and bale it, among hundreds of other tasks that used to be carried out by humans and horses. You can attach a front-end loader, a forage harvester, a baler and more. These days, you need a tractor to tend even a moderate-sized property.

Wayne Caldwell, a professor of rural planning in the School of Environmental Design and Rural Development at the University of Guelph, grew up on a farm in Ontario's Huron County. His dad worked about a hundred acres of mixed cash crops, growing some turnips and potatoes as well as raising livestock such as hogs and cattle. Caldwell, who was born in 1957, can just barely remember the time when his dad relied on horses and his own muscles to carry out the seasonal chores. "I can recall as a young child, Dad threshing with two other farmers. One of them was his cousin and the other was the man who lived down the road," he said. In those days, the hard work of farming was shared between the men in the community—they'd come to help Wayne's dad thresh his fields, and in return, Wayne's dad would help them get their hay off. Horses were used to pull the binder that cut the grain as well as the hay-loader used to lift the hay from the fields and onto the wagon that took it back to the barn. When Wayne was young, these horses were replaced by a tractor, and he grew up watching the change the machine brought to his family farm and his community. "My dad with the tractor and the equipment, he was much more independent than he would have been historically."

Although his dad never expanded his production by purchasing more acres like many of his neighbours, the new machinery made his work more manageable. He was able to increase his productivity, and that meant he was able to bring in the harvest more quickly and spend less time in the fields. And because he didn't need the horses any longer, there was space and feed to keep more cattle, which added to the family's income. So the tractor improved his family's quality of life. They went on holidays, bought a TV (around the same time, the countryside was electrified). For the neighbours with bigger and bigger farms, suddenly there was no limit to the amount of land one man could cultivate. And more land meant more crops, which, theoretically, meant more money.

Theoretically.

While farmers were suddenly able to tend more land, their costs rose with the increase in acreage. As demand for arable soil rose, the price per acre crept up in tandem with the amount of land one person was able to farm. The cost of this new machinery needed to till, plough and hay all this acreage was similarly high. Then there were the new chemical fertilizers and pesticides on the market—another bill—as well as new seed varieties to help squeeze out even higher yields from the soil but cost more money. This meant the farmer needed to farm even more land to grow more crops to pay his rising bills. But so did the neighbour, and the neighbour's neighbour and the neighbour's neighbour's neighbour. As a result, between 1945 and 1970, productivity on the Canadian farm rose by 6 percent a year. But the farmers didn't reap the benefits. As commodities flooded the market, the price of crops went down, following standard supply-and-demand theory. Now the farmer had to farm even *more* land to pay the bills. This continuing cycle of rising input costs and diminishing commodity prices has been labelled the cost-price squeeze.[7] Wayne's dad wasn't affected like others; nor were the neighbours who'd bought more land when the price wasn't so high. But the squeeze was felt by many other farmers across the country.

At the same time, now that Wayne's dad didn't need his neighbours' help in the same way, the social landscape of the rural community began to change. Up until grade four, Wayne attended a one-room schoolhouse, which was a walk away, but in the mid-sixties, the school board shut down the small rural school and started busing kids to the local village. Life in the country was fundamentally altered. No more were the days of barn raisings, and there weren't as many card parties. Instead of collaborating with their neighbours to get the work done, as people did in his dad's time, farmers now hire people when they need help. Every aspect of community life has changed. "Rural communities are still vibrant and connected, but they are different. The element of community that was historically there is no longer." Add to this the growing number of opportunities available to farm kids in the city—like the promise of post-secondary education that drew Wayne. The lure of farming no longer exists for those who traditionally went into agriculture. For young people, farming is no longer a job of choice.

But then that's not the whole story.

•

A new generation of people want to farm. Their parents are more likely to have been nurses or teachers or plumbers or engineers, but they are more interested in working the land than working for the man. Across Canada, farming is capturing the imagination of a growing group of men and women who have no recent ancestral connections to agriculture. These are the people who will likely play an important role in a new food system and make the idea of local food possible in Canada.

Farm internship programs are rising in popularity, like the Collaborative Regional Alliance for Farmer Training in Ontario. CRAFT matches aspiring farmers with organic farms in the hope of strengthening the organic farming community in the province. Applications for their two dozen internships have risen into the hundreds in the last few years. The international organization called WWOOF—World Wide Opportunities on Organic Farms—which facilitates volunteering on farms, has a Canadian membership that is growing exponentially, primarily with people in their twenties. John Vanden Heuvel, the founder of the Canadian chapter, said young families are starting to take their kids to work on farms in the summer too. Across the country, training programs are being launched for those drawn to agriculture but who don't have a farming background. The non-profit Agricultural Research and Extension Council of Alberta is starting courses to train future farmers because of the high demand for this service in the West. And they are basing their program on the work of yet another organization, FarmStart, in Ontario, that has been helping new farmers move into agriculture since 2002.

FarmStart, based in Guelph, was founded by a woman named Christie Young who had worked with farmers as well as in the community-food sector for years and saw a huge gap in the food system between aspiring farmers and the reality of farm life. She saw that there was little support for people who wanted to learn how to run their own operation. There wasn't an apprenticeship program like the ones for electricians or carpenters, in which someone at the beginning of their career works closely with a more experienced person to learn on the job before starting their own business. So she founded the not-for-profit FarmStart to help put more farmers into the fields with the skills and knowledge necessary to succeed.

Their focus is not only on getting new farmers out there growing food for Canadians. Christie Young wants to help the new inductees rethink agriculture in Canada and help them to create a more ecologically, and economically, sustainable way of farming. Those who register for the FarmStart courses tend to be people with university degrees, many from the environmental sciences, who are not only ideologically committed to sustainability but have a practical side that makes them good business managers. Young is hopeful that interest from this new segment of society can radically change the way food is produced. "Ecological agriculture is thinking about the farm as a whole system, basing it on soil health and looking at it differently," she said. "We've done some pretty serious things to the land. But I've seen farms turned around by someone who is concerned with building their soil."

To help this new generation accomplish these goals, FarmStart offers a wide range of services, such as technical courses on how to build soil naturally or business planning to help people figure out how to improve their profit margins. They also have an online land-matching system, farmlinkontario.ca, that puts landless farmers in touch with people and businesses (including real estate speculators who can sit on agricultural properties for decades) who want their land to produce food. They also teach immigrants who have an agricultural background, and wish to farm here, about Canadian agriculture. And they run two incubator farms where these new farmers can put their business plans in place and start to farm without taking on the initial risk and expense of buying land. One of these new farmers who has been very successful is Daniel Hoffmann, a vegetable grower who is working a two-acre plot at FarmStart's McVean Farm.

The McVean Farm is a beautiful farm. The fields are flat, the soil a rich clay loam. It's also lovely to look at, with an old wooden barn, some old apple trees and black walnuts where a flock of blue jays perched the day I visited. It also happens to be smack in the middle of urban sprawl, a sliver of farmland drowning amid newly constructed houses with multi-car garages and driveways the size of an ample market garden. Located at the edge of Toronto in the suburb of Brampton, the thirty-seven-acre farm is owned by the Toronto and Region Conservation Authority, which is likely the only reason this old farm, bought after 1954's Hurricane Hazel as part of a flood and soil erosion program, was never turned into a subdivision.

Daniel Hoffmann drives here about five times a week from the main-floor apartment he rents in midtown Toronto. In 2008, Hoffmann started the farming/social work operation he calls The Cutting Veg, which encompasses a variety of activities, including growing vegetables for two

Toronto-area farmers' markets, producing global varieties of seed garlic he sells to other farmers, and a sixty-eight-member CSA, as well as wellness counselling and food and garden consulting. Hoffmann hopes his business will promote social and environmental health and balance, not only by growing organic food for city folks but by providing them with an opportunity to nurture a connection to the land and to the food that nourishes them. He offers internships through which he trains people interested in farming in exchange for vegetables and draws on a large pool of volunteers who leave the farm after a work shift with food to eat.

Hoffmann grew up in the city and studied social work at university, but farming has called to him for years. After finishing his undergraduate degree, he ran an organic farm on Vancouver Island before moving to Toronto to work with adults with mental illness. He always felt, as a social worker, that food and farming had a healing element. Now he combines both his passions by feeding people organic food and helping those who wish to reconnect with the earth.

Compare the way Hoffmann farms with the traditional farmer ploughing the back fifty with his tractor. Both are legitimate. Both produce food. But how they approach what they do is so different. The new generation of people who are attracted to farming are redefining all aspects of it: the way they gain access to land, their cultivation techniques and the way they market their produce. Christie Young of FarmStart said the new farmers they see are more likely to farm ecologically than conventionally. Because they don't generally have access to large sums of capital and are wary of going into debt, they devise tractor-sharing schemes with their neighbours and other creative ways of getting the job done. "They approach the business model differently. They grow slower. They rent land. They grow higher-value crops on smaller acreages," said Young. When it comes to selling their produce, they tend to avoid the traditional supply chains and instead focus their marketing efforts on a specific community. Hoffmann, for one, drew on his Jewish cultural connections to start his

CSA. He called it Tikkun Adamah, which means "healing of the earth" in Hebrew, and used a Jewish educational garden in Vaughan as the CSA depot where members could pick up their produce. He has since been approached by another synagogue to grow for them as well. Because of his approach to farming, he has been successful. Not only has he contributed to the food chain but he's figured out how to make a living at it. "I've earned more this year than I ever did at any job," he said.

It's an Internet-generation approach to farming: looking to networks that are rooted in community for information sharing, equipment, marketing and sales. By rethinking how farmers earn a living and sell their food, these new farmers are creating a new kind of food system in which the connection between eater and farmer is strengthened and farmers are able to profit more from their work—which is not unlike what the Really Local Harvest Co-op has done in New Brunswick.

．

But city kids turned farmers aren't the only source of new ideas. This new generation of farmers comes not only from all walks of life but from every sector of society, every region of this country. Nova Scotia is one of the places the new farmers are heading because, outside of the Annapolis Valley, land here is relatively cheap—at least compared with what it costs to buy a farm in Ontario or British Columbia. People who haven't had family help and didn't grow up on the farm are starting out in this province. On a small scale, it's a farming lab, an incubator province where new farmers can make a go of it.

Rupert Jannasch is one of these new farmers. His place is called Ironwood Farm, and it is found on the Hants shore in Nova Scotia, not too far from Windsor and the ocean. To drive there is to navigate a maze of winding roads with turnoffs here and there and few street signs; it's quite the trip. But it was well worth the effort. Ironwood Farm is stunning, with a ramshackle house and an antique barn and land that straddles the road. If you cross over in front of the house and make your way into some of Jannasch's best vegetable land, you can see the Avon River at the foot of his fields. Jannasch is a beginner farmer, though at forty-six he's not exactly young to be starting a new career. He bought the land in 2004 to start an organic farm. He grows blueberries and raspberries and, in a greenhouse he constructed, he raises market vegetables such as spinach, lettuce and tomatoes. In the field across the road, he grows field tomatoes, sweet potatoes and squash.

Although he had never owned his own farm, Jannasch has been working in agriculture most of his life, ever since the summer he was sixteen and his dad gave him a choice between working on a farm or with the coast guard. He chose the farm and spent the warm months working with hogs. Ever since, he has dabbled in the field, travelling the world to work in Germany, Israel, New Zealand, as well as in western Canada. But it wasn't until he was forty-two that he decided to buy a farm of his own.

Jannasch's take on farming is an unconventional one. To begin with, he didn't approach the bank for help buying his land. Instead, a not-for-profit organization gave him money to buy the land in return for the development rights and a conservation easement on about 150 acres. It's a win-win arrangement: Jannasch got his farm, and the organization fulfilled its environmental mandate by protecting the land and ensuring that no one will ever be able to build there or clear-cut.

"That first summer and fall I spent just looking around me at the immensity of the project I'd taken on," he remembered. The farm had been idle for several years, its elderly owner no longer able to keep it in production. Jannasch had to decide what to do with the old outbuildings, learn to work the two Massey Ferguson tractors that came with the place and decide what he wanted to produce. So far, it has been going well enough. The first two years he didn't make a profit, but things improved a little after that. A friend from down the road sells Jannasch's berries and tomatoes at the Halifax Farmers' Market along with his own crops, and

Jannasch has a U-pick for his raspberries and blueberries. He has hired some locals to help him out—including a very slim man named Brent, who cycles out to the farm from Halifax, a four- to six-hour ride depending on the winds, to work a few days a week.

Jannasch tries to balance a sound business model with his ecological approach to farming. "It has to be ecologically and financially sound," he said. But this is a challenge, because to make more money, he would need to produce more, and that would mean taking on debt to invest in infrastructure to increase his yields. If he were to do this, he would end up mimicking the very conventional farms he defines himself against. So he is trying to find a way to balance financial vitality with environmentalism. "My biggest goal would be that in twenty years or so someone would be prepared to take on the work that I've started," he said.

Jannasch is not the only one in the area who has an alternative approach to farming. It seems that a number of these new arrivals have their own take on what it means to farm. Not too far away from Jannasch's is Sunroot Organic Farms, a co-operative project run by a group of friends. They are originally from Ontario, where they found the price of land to be prohibitive, and so they looked east for their hundred acres. Instead of selling their produce to whomever wants to buy it, they've decided to try to feed their community. They started an organic-vegetable CSA for about fifty families and applied for government funding so they could offer their food to low-income people in the area.

Jannasch acknowledges that these kinds of farms are small—in his case, there really is only so much you can do as one man farming on your own. While he and his neighbours may not be feeding thousands of people, they are transforming agriculture as we've known it. "It's a very interesting question what new farmers are contributing to the food system," he said. "It's very easy to criticize the attempt of small-scale farms, but because of their scale, in the long run, they may be around much longer than what people call the 'real farms.'"

•

It's not only the new people who are farming differently in Nova Scotia. Some younger people who grew up on the farm and saw their parents working hard for little reward are also rethinking the traditional agricultural model. As it turns out, embracing change can pay off.

These days, Greg and Suzanne are doing well. Finally. "It makes us a living," Greg said. "We live okay right now. Whether we are rich or not, that's a matter of interpretation." They took a vacation to Jamaica last winter and are planning two weeks away again this year. Suzanne also has plans for the house. She wants to move the front door so that people enter into where the living room is today and put the office at the side so men with muddy boots (read Greg) don't trek dirt through the living area. The kitchen will get a facelift too. They also want to reduce the ecological footprint of the farm by installing a subterranean heating and cooling system for the greenhouse, which could cost a fair sum, but the idea of getting off the grid appeals to Greg.

The secret of their success, he said, is direct marketing. They stopped selling to the chains and instead they now sell directly to their customers at the Halifax Farmers' Market, at a couple of other markets in the area, as well as to the neighbouring farms that run their own roadside stands stocking foods from the Annapolis Valley. "The first year we stopped growing vegetables for stores was the first year we made money in the vegetable business," said Greg. While they may be making a profit, it's still not easy. There's demand, but the prices customers are willing to pay remain low, keeping the profits down, and he's scared to raise the price because of the competition from supermarkets. Greg can tell when there's a sale on broccoli there, for example, because he notices a definite dip in their sales at that week's market.

Even though the farm is prospering, I got the sense that something about farming is eating away at Greg. The way he paused and looked off into the distance, the reluctant tone of his voice, led me to believe that something was frustrating him. Then he explained to me that it is the lack of respect he is afforded by society. "I saw a TV show and kids were insulting each other by calling them farmers. I was like, No!" As he told me this, he raised his hands to his head in disbelief, tugging on his hair, his face contorting in obvious agony. "Running a farm of this size and this complexity is about as hard as running Nova Scotia Power. But I don't get the $5-million bonuses." He would like to hire some people from the area to work alongside him, possibly even a foreman to take over some of the management, but it's been difficult to find the right person who is willing to take on the responsibility.

"You can't get the locals to do anything," he said. "There's a stigma. I'm sure there are people who would love to. But they don't want to be seen as working on a farm." So Greg and Suzanne fly in workers from the Caribbean. I can't help but think about that ecological footprint. Also, many of the migrant workers are farmers in their own countries, but are unable to make a living at home. There is much debate about the ethics of luring doctors from the third world to come to Canada. What about farmers? How sustainable is our food system if we poach labour and know-how from poorer countries? For our local food system to flourish, everybody who works on the farm, from the labourer to the farmer who owns the land, should be respected and paid well. "Your salary is inversely related to the service you provide society," said Greg. "Hockey players make money and the farmer makes pennies."

That said, he thinks their new sales strategy might be the secret to financial stability. "What we are doing is going back to the way it was done a hundred years ago. It's only in the last few generations that there's been the huge, long industrial food chain that puts the farmer last. Really, we've gone back to basics, that's all we've done. It's made a difference between having an agriculture income or not. The size of farm we have, we would not be in business if we didn't do it the way we are doing it. We've beaten the odds. Our only income comes from the farm, and there are very few farms in Canada that do that. And we're living as well as the next guy." For what they've accomplished, the Nova Scotia Institute of Agrologists awarded Greg and Suzanne the Outstanding Farm Family Award for 2009.

·

Ten minutes down the road from Greg and Suzanne's place in the Annapolis Valley is their friend Patricia Bishop's farm. At thirty-three, she is a young farmer but not a new arrival on the farm—she jokes that she and her husband, Josh Oulton, both learned to farm, walk and talk as babies. They each come from old Nova Scotia farming stock. Patricia's ancestors arrived in the area from Connecticut back in the 1700s, and she grew up watching her extended family make a decent living farming at Noggins Corner—the intersection where the family farm is headquartered was once the place to stop for noggins of rum, hence the name. Her family runs a successful roadside stand—what they call a farm market in Nova Scotia—where they sell fresh produce directly to the consumer. Josh's grandparents brought the first Charolais beef cows to the area from France in the 1900s, and he too was raised on the farm.

Bishop is representative of the way the new generation of farmers can break from their parents' tradition. Recently, the couple, who have three young children, bought their own small organic farm, which they call TapRoot Farms. It's made up of eight acres of certified organic gardens where they grow a range of vegetables, including beans, radishes, lettuce, zucchini, squash, basil, strawberries, garlic and much more. Even though Bishop's family is known in the area for being a successful farming family, with multiple farms and many acres under cultivation, she and Josh are approaching the family trade in a new way. They have started a CSA, providing weekly organic boxes to people in Dartmouth and Halifax all year round, about which Bishop blogs, posting many photos online.

While Greg Gerrits is concerned about a lack of respect for farming that keeps their peers out of the fields, Patricia Bishop worries about her generation's access to agricultural land. Within minutes of arriving at her place, she suggests we go for a drive. She's very concerned about the competition for property between farmers and people from the city who love this area and have the money to outbid any new farmers like herself—so concerned that she made the issue the cornerstone of her campaign when she ran for municipal office in 2008. (She lost by a small margin.)

We jumped into the truck, the gravel of the driveway scattering as she accelerated. There was a car seat in the back for one of her kids, and a plastic toy at my feet. We headed down the paved road, past the Minas Basin and the Wellington Dyke, with its gorgeous red sand and greying tall grasses, to the prime vegetable fields on its banks. It's flat, south-facing— Bishop pointed to it as she drove, calling it "beautiful agricultural land." But right in the middle of the plot was a big house with a two-car garage and a manicured lawn. Along the road, the same sight is repeated again and again.

As Bishop talked about this residential encroachment on agricultural land, her voice seized, belying a tension that exists not only in the Annapolis Valley but across the country wherever farms are being turned into recreational properties. "You wave to each other, you talk to each other," said Bishop of her new neighbours, "but you never have the conversation: Why did you choose to build your house on agricultural land? It's hard," she said, meaning how challenging it is for younger people to get into farming and buy property. "You need a lot of acreage." She's worried because her peers, the kids she grew up with who, like her, were steeped in agricultural know-how as children, are leaving the province in droves. "There are people who want to farm but they don't because it doesn't make financial sense."

I left the Annapolis Valley feeling confused. There is so much excitement in the changes the new farmers are introducing. But many hurdles remain too, as both Greg Gerrits and Patricia Bishop pointed out. I didn't know whether to be hopeful or worried about the future.

. . .

If there is ever some serious hope for the future, it can be found at Everdale Organic Farm and Environmental Learning Centre. Everdale is a non-profit organization that is part farm (they run a CSA and sell the produce they grow at farmers' markets) and part educational project (they offer farming and environmental programming for kids and adults). And every year since 2000, they have been helping to train aspiring farmers. A handful of people are selected to live on the farm and work for almost nothing (they receive $90 a month) in return for the opportunity to learn how to farm organically and run a viable business. It's not just the young and the idealistic who apply. A number of people who are mid-career and mid-life have come to Everdale in search of a new path. One of them is Brenda Hsueh.

From a distance, Brenda looked different from the other farm interns. Her yellow rain jacket was pulled straight down over her black rain pants, which fell perfectly over her rubber boots. Her hair was tied back into a neat ponytail and she was wearing navy blue earmuffs. Her eyeglasses kept slipping down her nose, but Brenda, gloved hands muddy and wet, expertly tipped her head back and the glasses slid back into place.

It was cold, it was wet, you could see your breath, but Brenda was unfazed. I shivered, clutched my pen and tried to keep up with her as she marched forward to join the other interns. They were finishing packing a row of carrots into bins before heading back to the main cabin for lunch.

Until a few months ago, Brenda worked in the financial industry. For seven years, she worked for a bond-rating agency in the fixed-income markets, walking to work every day from her condominium near Toronto's Rogers Centre to her cubicle in a big office tower downtown. She liked her job, had a group of good friends she met regularly for dinner on Queen Street, and enjoyed living in the middle of the city, yet she was nagged by a dream she couldn't shake. Brenda wanted to be a farmer, "a practitioner of sustainable agriculture." She yearned for the land even though she had grown up first in suburban Edmonton and then in Mississauga. She is the child of Taiwanese immigrants, an engineer and a lab technician who had no background in agriculture, and yet she was drawn to farming. When she was laid off in the spring of 2008, rather than look for another job in the financial industry, she decided it was time to start on her new path. She came to Everdale, where she hoped to gain enough hands-on experience to help her start her own organic farm. She spent the summer weeding beds and harvesting kale, celery, radishes, and beans, all the while living at first in a tent for five weeks and then in a cabin on the Everdale property. She loved every moment.

"When I go back to Toronto," said Brenda, "my friends can't believe how happy I am. It's not that I was unhappy before. I liked my job. I feel like I've answered my calling in sustainable agriculture. My friends are all like, Really? You want to do this? They are still in shock that I'm here." She then told me about her ongoing hunt for the right piece of property that she planned to finance with the sale of her condo.

I spent the morning at Everdale, shivering while I interviewed the aspiring farmers as they picked vegetables. Despite the cold, the damp and the frost that had damaged most of the chard, I felt the allure of what they were doing. They brimmed with passion for the work they had only recently discovered. Another one of the interns, a thirty-four-year-old man named Simeron Novak, also had an entirely different career until that summer. He worked as an oysterman on Toronto's dining scene during the height of the economic boom, when much money was spent on high-priced restaurant meals. But he left it all behind, disgusted by the waste he saw, and dreamt instead of starting his own farm where he would grow hops and possibly even start a microbrewery.

A voice crackled over the walkie-talkie and announced that lunch was ready. I followed the group and climbed with them into the cab of the old pickup truck with years of dirt engrained in its maroon vinyl bench seats. As we bumped back over the field, I marvelled at the future.

Imagine what would happen if these people from many different professional backgrounds with varying experiences actually have the opportunity to farm. What an impact this burst of creativity could have. Already we're seeing how a new generation is changing agriculture and is helping to build a new local and sustainable food system here. If tens, hundreds, thousands of new people are drawn into the fields, imagine how different our food system could be.

CHAPTER THREE

BEYOND WHEAT

Organics, Climate Change and a New Way in Saskatchewan

Saskatoon's grain elevators are so big you can see them from the other side of town. Twenty cylindrical towers forty metres tall, attached one to the other like a giant hive, stand in a field on the western edge of the city. This complex is one of the two largest inland grain elevators on the continent, the nexus in an elaborate distribution system that processes wheat, barley, lentils, field peas, oats, mustard, flax and other oilseeds and pulses from the farmers' fields in Saskatoon and ships the commodities to thousands of points around the globe. Within a few days this place can put lentils that were grown in the province onto a train and send them to a distant port where they are then loaded onto a boat and carried as far away as India. The grain elevator also sends canola to China and Pakistan, wheat to South America and birdseed to feed New York City's pets—rumour in the business has it that New Yorkers go through one railcar of the stuff a day.

The efficiency of the industrial food system is awe-inspiring.

Standing at the foot of the grain elevators, I could hear the machines churning inside. It was an eerie sound, a mechanical hum with an unrelenting pulsing—twang, twang, twang, twang. The sky was purple, the colour of an early-winter morning on the Prairies, but the shadow where I was standing at the base of the enormous elevator was deep and dark. A CP train had pulled up on the tracks that lead into a sheltered area attached to the towers, to be loaded with a shipment of grain. Its cars were spray-painted with graffiti that in today's globalized food system act like labels on an old steamer trunk; they offer a clue to how far the train has come and the distance the grain will travel, just as soon as the men load it up.

Export agriculture is the spine of Saskatchewan's economy. The province exports more than a billion dollars' worth of grain a year. It's the antithesis of a local food system. This province feeds the world. The day I visited the head office, in a small building next to the grain elevators, they were preparing for a shipment to Mexico.

"Brett!" shouted Sheldon Hahn, the operations manager, from inside his office, as he put down the phone. "Hey, Dogger!" A big man wearing coveralls and workboots stuck his head in the door. "SGS"—a company that does grain-quality grading—"requires samples on the Mexico train," Hahn told him.

"For which shipment?"

"Twenty-five to Mexico."

"Oh, Mexico. Hey, when's that going out?"

"Friday. But that CN is also going out on Friday. So who knows."

It's complicated, trying to juggle receiving with distribution. Incoming grain requires grading. Before each load is stored in the grain elevators or shipped to its next stop on the food chain, the workers here must measure the amount of dockage (plant stalks and other detritus) that invariably is mixed in, the quality of the grain and its protein content. Then the grain that will leave the facility is loaded onto boxcars or transport trucks. The outgoing vehicles, long-distance trains and fourteen-wheeler trucks, arrive at all hours of the day and night. The grain elevator has the capacity to load between 100 and 112 railcars a day. It doesn't stop. For most of the year, it works twenty-four hours straight, with grain moving constantly through the place. The process is necessarily speedy, to ensure that the lentils make it to port in time to catch the ship, or that the canola is loaded onto a truck to cross the Prairies before the plant requires its next load to press into oil. Or so the Mexicans get their wheat. Now that's a lot of fast-moving food.

The cycle starts when the trucks or boxcars, filled to the brim with the harvest and travelling from central collection points across the province, pull up to the grain elevator. The vehicle is positioned over a pit in a garage-like area attached to the main building and the load is dumped into the hopper below. A conveyor belt moves the newly arrived shipment into the basement of the grain elevators, at which point small buckets, bolted onto a different conveyor belt, scoop the grains and whisk them nearly fifty metres up the tower. The belt moves quickly.

The air was thick with a yellow haze of grain dust when Hahn and I entered the grain elevator. I choked on the air, hiding my face in my scarf, trying not to breathe it in. We took an elevator to meet the golden blur of grain at the top. The buckets flipped over and dumped their contents into another channel. First, the shipment needed to be weighed. Hahn explained that this was the only point at which the grain is motionless between the time it is dropped into the hopper and when it lands at its final destination. We stood there, waiting for the cycle to stop for a few seconds while the scale recorded the weight and then watched as the grain started to move again—on its way to port, to a malt plant or a brewery, or an ethanol plant, a feedlot or a flour mill.

What I witnessed at the grain elevator hasn't changed much in a hundred years, though computers and machines carry out what men used to do by heaving and pulling on thick ropes. The federal government built these elevators in 1914 to help move the grain from the Prairies out into the world. It has worked really well. Canada is one of the top five wheat-producing countries in the world. There's a reason they call the Prairies a breadbasket.

Farming today in Saskatchewan is best described as big business. In 1921, the average size of a farm in the province was 369 acres. By 1956, that had risen to an average of 607 acres. The size has increased steadily, and today in Saskatchewan, the average farm is 1,450 acres, with many as large as several thousand acres. These fields are planted with grains and oilseeds to be sold on the commodities markets. Wheat is the most ubiquitous crop, followed by coarse grains like barley and oats and oilseeds like canola and flax, then the pulses (chickpeas, lentils, beans). The Canadian Wheat Board, the largest wheat-marketing agency in the world, is responsible for selling wheat and barley on behalf of about 75,000 Canadian farmers. The board acts as the go-between, arranging sales between farmers and buyers, both at home and abroad.

The wheat board, the mega-farms, the grain elevators—these are all important components of the global food system. These various parts work together to satisfy the world's hunger for wheat. Most of humanity still relies primarily on foods made from grains like wheat, rice and corn. People around the world depend on grains for about half of their calories. Farmers have never grown so much of the stuff, and yields today are at a historic high. In 1961, the amount of grain grown per person worldwide was 285 kilograms; now this number is about 350 kilos, representing a tripling of the grain supply during a period when the population doubled.[8] Demand for these commodities continues to surge because industrial livestock production is now being practised in countries like India, increasing the need for corn and soybeans to feed to the animals. Ethanol production has also started to compete for this finite supply of grains. That grain tower in Saskatoon plays an important role.

Nevertheless, a small but growing group of people reject this model of agriculture. They say the system is broken, and they propose an alternative that is based on a local-food model rather than a global and industrial one. Some farmers in Saskatchewan are abandoning the mainstream food system, creating an alternative on the Prairies and showing that local is possible, even in these parts.

.

From the sidewalk out front of Wilma Pool's house, in the middle of Saskatoon, if you turn to face west, on the horizon you can see the grain elevators. They are a constant reminder of the food system that Pool, a farmer named Keith Neu and a small group of people in this city are trying to circumvent. In the garage off the alley round the back of the house, they are building an entirely different, extremely local food-distribution system. This garage, with two deep-freezes, a wood stove for warmth in the winter and some space to hang around and chat on Saturday mornings amid the jumble of odds and ends in storage, is a central hub in one of the many spokes of a new food economy in Saskatchewan.

Once a month, Keith Neu sets out from his 1,400-acre farm up in Hudson Bay, a small town near the Manitoba border, and drives three and a half hours into the city. His old white delivery truck pulls in around 10 a.m., loaded with eggs, vegetables, fruit and meat that he and his family have grown and prepared on their farm for the two dozen families who belong to his CSA. Members of a community-supported agriculture scheme usually expect a season's worth of fresh produce when they hand over their cash to secure their share of the farmer's crop, but this wasn't the case the first year Keith started his CSA. In 2007, it was the farm's bad fortune the members shared, rather than vegetables, when wet weather destroyed his crops. "It was the year from hell," said Keith, remembering the rains that drowned the fields. He was able to offer almost nothing to his members. Some people dropped out. It cost them $100 a month that season, and they received little food in return. Those who stayed did it for the big picture. They understood that they were helping the farmer and knew that if he could make a go of it, maybe they would be helping to create a new way in the Prairies.

Keith, too, is committed to creating something different. "I don't believe in grain," he said matter-of-factly. This comment may be sacrilege in the province, but Keith is an outspoken man who is highly politicized, and who believes deeply in what he stands for: the small farmer, not the corporations he fears are destroying the food system. He regularly comes out with pithy one-liners that take a stab at the food system he's proudly divorced himself from. "It's out of the whole commercial food web," he said to me. "The only way to be food secure is to be out of the system." Later, he added: "I've got vegetables. I've got meat. I've got the full meal deal." Regarding grain, he does grow some on his farm and offers it as part of the CSA. It is commodity grain that he's against, the stuff that cycles through the grain elevators, with its high environmental costs.

Keith has been farming since he was fourteen, when he joined his dad on the family farm, about twenty-five kilometres away from where they are today. His father grew up during the Depression, when drought plagued Saskatchewan, and has seen tough times on the Prairies. So has his son. Keith bought his first farm in the early 1980s and went to work as a commodity farmer, growing grains like most farmers in Saskatchewan. But those were the days of soaring interest rates and the beginning of the farm crisis that saw farm after farm shut down across the country as farmers couldn't pay their bills because they were selling their crops for less than the cost of production. In 1989, Keith declared bankruptcy and lost his eight hundred acres of farmland. With no land, he had no choice but to leave farming, and he went to work in construction and in the Alberta oil refineries. It wasn't until after he met his wife that he moved back to Saskatchewan to return to the land and take over his dad's farm.

It was his wife who got him into beef. She had grown up on a ranch, and her dad encouraged them to move into cattle. Keith became an organic farmer because of his own dad, who had gone organic in the 1980s when he decided he didn't want to pay the big bills for chemical fertilizers and pesticides. When Keith started raising cattle, he kept them organically too. "We said: 'Let's stop feeding the chemical companies and let's feed ourselves.'" For the next fifteen years he ran a mixed organic farm. Then, his life turned another corner at a local meeting for people concerned about food security in the area. He looked around and saw that he was the only farmer in the room. "I'm thinking, Shit, I can *grow* food. Why am I going to the store to buy crap when I'm an organic farmer?" The next year, he started a five-acre market garden with plans to expand. By 2009, it covered eight acres.

The system that Keith has created is ingenious, a true partnership between the community and the farm. To join his CSA, it costs $120 a month for the grain and vegetables he grows on the farm. Members are encouraged to tell him in the spring what they like to eat so he can cater to their tastes. All season long, people receive their share of the harvest, and the extra produce is frozen on the farm in a professional facility so that for the rest of the year, they can continue to eat Keith's vegetables. He sells the beef at a cost of $4.50 a pound, and a seven-pound chicken costs $20. But it's the way he approaches the egg production that makes me think that he's really on to something new. He charges a $50 one-time payment that he uses to buy chicks so you actually own your laying hen. Members subsidize the chick's upkeep for the six months they require to mature, and once the hen starts to lay, Keith charges $2.50 a dozen for the organic eggs.

Keith has big plans. He wants to keep bees for honey, and he plans to make prepared foods like soups and stews as well as sell the farm's home canning. He also hopes to eventually build an on-farm abattoir so the cattle he kills himself won't have to be driven hundreds of kilometres for processing in a regulated facility. (He goes into the barn with a gun and pats the cows tenderly before shooting them in the head, the most humane way possible, he said.) He'd like to do all this just as soon as he can recruit enough members for his scheme. "I'm doing this stuff in desperation. How am I going to keep farming and make a living?"

But he's fully convinced that organic, community-based agriculture is the way to go. Keith's farming is about sustainable agriculture, farming in a way that minimizes the impact on the earth. His move away from petrochemical pesticides and fertilizers reduces his carbon load, and because he runs a mixed farm, where he grows crops and raises livestock, he is able to cycle nutrients on the farm. He is the steward of the nutrient loop. It's a natural metabolism: the cows eat grass, providing manure to fertilize the crops as well as meat for human consumption. The pasture where the cows eat is fertilized by the animals themselves, and then worms, nematodes and other tiny organisms help turn the manure into rich soil, which encourages more grass growth. The cows eat the grass and the cycle continues.

.

Some might take issue with Keith's claim that his farm is better for the earth. In the last few years, a debate about food miles has erupted in the media. James E. McWilliams, an associate professor at Texas State University and author of *Just Food: Where Locavores Get It Wrong and How We Can Truly Eat Responsibly*, is one of a handful of academics who have come forward to denounce the idea that buying local food is better for the environment than buying food grown in an efficient industrial system and shipped to a supermarket near you. They argue that because transportation represents only a small percentage of the carbon load of food, it is foolish to rely on geography alone when making a decision about what to buy. "There are areas of the world that are naturally inclined to produce more food," McWilliams told me. "We should try to support the development of food systems in these regions." He argues for improvements in transportation to lower the environmental impact of moving food from where it was produced to where it is consumed.

The most reported example of the refutation of local food comes from New Zealand, where one study found that lamb grown and raised in the United Kingdom has a larger carbon footprint than New Zealand lamb that is shipped to British supermarkets. The study, out of Lincoln University, found that every tonne of meat raised in their country produced 688 kilograms of carbon dioxide compared with 2,849 kilograms for British lamb. (Their results were similar for apples grown in the two countries.) The New Zealand emissions were lower for lamb, the authors concluded, because the animals graze year-round in that country and farmers there employ less energy-intensive fertilizers. The study did come under attack because of the authors' connections to agribusiness, and academics disputed the numbers. It was also criticized for not factoring in the carbon emissions of transportation within New Zealand and the U.K. In addition, critics suggested that the conclusions would have been different had the study compared the New Zealand lamb to British sheep raised on farms that practise sustainable agriculture and sell their meat locally. However, this study's fundamental argument that food miles are not a good way to measure environmental cost has credence.

Pierre Desrochers, a geography professor at the University of Toronto Mississauga, also dispels the assumption that food miles constitute a large part of the carbon load of the food system. In a 2009 study published by the Mercatus Center at George Mason University, he wrote that food miles are "at best, a marketing fad that frequently and severely distorts the environmental impacts of agricultural production." He and his wife, Hiroko Shimizu, who co-authored the paper, hold that the problem with food miles is that they distract the consumer from the benefits of industrial agriculture. "I believe our modern agribusiness system is the result of the most efficient producers using resources the most efficiently," he said to me. "Yes, there are problems. But overall, the problems don't outweigh the benefits of the modern agricultural system." Under benefits he lists the fact that we as a society are free from subsistence agriculture (he grew up in rural Quebec and witnessed first-hand what he saw to be the drudgery of farming, saying, "I was always jealous of suburban kids"). He also praises the speed and efficiency of the industrial model that brings us cheap and abundant food, and he holds that the globalization of the food system creates jobs for people participating in export agriculture in countries like Kenya and Mexico. (It should be noted that the Mercatus Center that published his research paper is a think tank funded largely by Koch Industries, an oil conglomerate. However, the centre's mandate clearly states that it "does not engage in research or educational activities directed or influenced in any way by financial supporters.")

Food miles alone aren't the best way to evaluate a food's environmental cost; I agree with this premise. However, in their calculations, Desrochers and his peers have missed the point. While it might be more efficient in terms of carbon emissions to grow five hundred acres of tomatoes in a Mexican field and drive them across the continent rather than growing tomatoes in a coal-fired greenhouse in Ontario, this debate about food miles ignores the bigger picture. What's more pertinent to the discussion is whether industrial agriculture is sustainable. The larger question the food miles debate demands of us is whether a global, industrial agricultural system is the best way to feed the planet. Can humanity continue to farm this way into the future, extracting the same yields without destroying the integrity of the environment?

I'd hazard a no. The ecological impact of industrial agriculture is wide and far reaching. To work this kind of farm in Saskatchewan, for example, you need many external inputs. Farmers require large tractors to handle extensive acreages, and an assortment of other equipment such as seeders and sprayers that run on fossil fuels. Then there are the chemicals that the vast monocultures depend on, like synthetic fertilizers, pesticides and herbicides. There's no time in industrial agriculture to use cover crops to build a field's fertility, like Keith Neu and other organic farmers take the time to do, because this would require letting some land lie fallow every year. Conventional farmers instead use nitrogen derived from natural gas, potassium from potash, and other elements like calcium and phosphorus to increase the fertility of the soil.[9] The monocultures of industrial agriculture are susceptible to pests, and so farmers are dependent on chemical pesticides. Genetically modified crops also require chemical products. Virtually all canola is genetically modified, such as Roundup Ready canola, which is engineered by Monsanto to be resistant to herbicide sprays, meaning that fields must be treated with chemicals. Then irrigation draws on dwindling water supplies and employs energy to pump the water from the source to the final destination. Farmers in Saskatchewan alone irrigate 169,625 acres of land.

All these inputs have helped farmers to grow more and more grains— we can thank the Green Revolution for these chemicals, as well as new hybrid varieties of grain bred by scientists that have boosted yields. Two countries in particular, Mexico and India, have benefited from the technology. Before the Green Revolution, neither was able to feed its own population from the domestic harvest. After widespread adoption of these techniques, both India and Mexico could feed themselves. Earlier, India was regularly plagued by famine, but there hasn't been one since the Green Revolution was initiated.

Those who believe in the industrial food system, as Desrochers does, hold that we need this kind of agriculture if we are to feed the world's growing population in the future. However, the environmental cost of the Green Revolution has been huge, as is argued by the likes of Vandana Shiva and Raj Patel. The high price of chemical inputs has left farmers in other countries facing farm crises there too. Pesticides have polluted the groundwater and the environment. Food-miles refuseniks often point to third world production as an environmentally friendly type of farming because in countries where labour costs are low, farmers replace the high-cost technological inputs such as tractors with human sweat. But even in countries like Kenya, which grows vegetables such as green beans for the European market, and Mexico, which supplies fresh foods such as zucchini and tomatoes to North America, there is a dependence on fossil fuels and chemicals as well as mass-scale irrigation that is destroying the environment.

Even those jobs in export agriculture that Desrochers praises are often of dubious benefit. According to Roni Neff, research and policy director at the Center for a Livable Future, at Johns Hopkins Bloomberg School of Public Health, an academic institute with a mandate to improve human health and feed the world's growing population in a sustainable way, agricultural jobs can come at a high cost in developing countries. Workers often work in unsafe conditions. For example, they can be exposed to chemicals such as pesticides without the protection they would have here in Canada. Often, the agricultural land and farming labour that would have supplied people with food locally is taken over by export agriculture, and the locals are left eating imported and processed foods. As well, there is a fragility built into the system. The jobs providing people with income aren't secure in the global marketplace. The corporation can decide to pick up shop, source the food elsewhere and suddenly leave people jobless—not unlike what happened with Brussels sprouts in Dieppe.

In Canada, too, the resource-intensive methods of agriculture that are satisfying the demand for grain come at an ecological cost. Industrial agriculture causes such problems as soil erosion, chemical contamination of our natural environment by fertilizers and pesticides, reduced biodiversity and overtaxed groundwater resources. Then there's the ratio of energy inputs into industrial agriculture to caloric energy we get out of the food grown this way. Today, we actually expend more energy growing crops than we get out of the harvest—in North America, it takes approximately two units of fossil fuels to harvest one unit of energy captured from the sun by the plant. This type of agriculture draws on more of the earth's resources than it puts back in—it uses more calories than it produces, and at the same time sucks up water from the earth at a faster rate than nature can replenish it. It is neither resilient nor sustainable. Laszlo Pinter, a director at the International Institute for Sustainable

Development, a Canadian policy research institute, said that, considering the social and environmental costs of the way we do things currently, we would all be better off in a world of local food systems.

.

People are trying in several ways to understand and quantify the effect of the industrial food system on the environment. Life cycle assessment (LCA), also known as cradle-to-grave analysis, breaks down the environmental costs at each stage of food production. LCA is the statistical quantification of the environmental impact of a product. All inputs are calculated, from a product's inception to its disposal. This technique is popular in Europe and the U.K., where it is used to distill a clearer picture of the true environmental costs of food production.

Researchers use LCA to determine, for example, the ecological cost of a hamburger. To do this, they look at the agricultural stage, the processing stage and then the marketing, consumption and disposal stages and add up all the inputs.[10] To raise beef, you need water, forage and, since most beef is raised in a feedlot, grains such as corn. Grain is grown using water and, if it is not organic, petroleum-based chemical fertilizer and pesticides. It requires tractors for seeding and harvesting and then trucks to transport it to the feedlot. The cattle themselves take an ecological toll because they produce methane (though exactly how much depends on the time of year, the quality of their pasture and whether they are fed grains). If you are conducting a cradle-to-grave analysis of a fast-food hamburger, then you factor in the bun (more cereal crops and all the resources required to raise them), with tomato, lettuce and onion, as well as mustard seeds, cucumbers and tomatoes for the condiments (yet more agricultural inputs as farmers grow these vegetables and truck them to a buyer).

At the processing stage, the cattle must be slaughtered (electricity, equipment), then butchered and ground. The wheat for the bun is milled into flour and then baked into buns. The mustard seeds, cucumbers and tomatoes for the mustard, relish and ketchup will be processed and then packaged in petroleum-based plastics. The various components of the burger are then processed, transported to a central distribution centre and then to the fast-food outlet where you will eat your lunch. Finally, the food is cooked using more energy, wrapped in some sort of package and then served to you. When you are finished your meal, you throw out what you didn't eat and discard the packaging, and the life cycle is complete.

To help provide perspective, those who practise cradle-to-grave analysis will often compare the life cycles of different methods of production to assess the tradeoffs a consumer makes when choosing to buy one food over another. A German study looked at what kind of bread used the least fossil fuels: organic or conventional, baked in a factory, a small bakery or in an electric bread-maker at home. It concluded that organic agriculture was preferable to conventional agriculture because it didn't use chemical fertilizers or pesticides and, therefore, used less energy. (However, the study did note that organic agriculture employs more land area because of crop-rotation requirements.) The factory turned the organic flour into one kilogram of bread most efficiently, while the home bread machine was the least efficient. The kicker of the study was that any benefits of choosing an organic factory-baked loaf were rendered nominal if you drove more than a kilometre to the store to buy the bread, because the greenhouse gas emissions of your car would eliminate the benefits of a more energy-efficient bread.

Life cycle assessment reveals in detail how the food system draws on a large number of resources. As a consumer, I found LCA made it more difficult to shop for food because it is hard to know how to interpret all the information it reveals. (Though I was relieved to learn from another LCA study, this one out of Switzerland, that consumers who are ecologically minded in their shopping actually have less of an environmental impact than what the authors called the "anti-ecologists," or those folks who just don't factor in the environment when making their food choices.[11])

Our food system doesn't look any more sustainable using another method of quantifying our demands on Mother Nature. The "ecological footprint" was developed in the 1980s by William Rees, a professor at the University of British Columbia, and Mathis Wackernagel, a graduate student at the time. The two measured human demand on the earth's biocapacity—that is, how much of the earth's natural resources we use—by translating our demands on nature into acres of land to paint a clear picture of how much of the earth's fixed resources we use. It can help to assess the ecological burden of our food system by calculating how much land area is needed to feed a society. As with LCA, the concept of the ecological footprint helps us to understand what we need to support our modern lifestyle and, in turn, makes it easier for us to determine how we can change the way we live so we can eat within our ecological means.

The ecological footprint is now widely accepted and is used by scientists, governments and organizations such as the World Wildlife Fund. It turns out that since the 1980s, we have been using far more of the earth's resources than the earth can regenerate, creating an environmental debt. According to the WWF's Living Planet Report, which puts numbers to humanity's use of natural resources, Canadians have one of the largest ecological footprints per capita in the world. We use 4.5 global acres of cropland per person, compared with France's 3.16 acres and Mexico's 1.9. If everyone were to eat like we do, it would take three planets' worth of available cropland to keep the world fed. Canadians also draw on more grazing land and fishing grounds than other countries.[12] Even though Canada has acres of arable land and a lot of clean water and forests, we as a country are nevertheless using more of the world's resources than we should if we as a species wish to live in a sustainable way.

No matter how you measure it, with either cradle-to-grave analysis or the ecological footprint, the Canadian food system is unsustainable. We have lived on cheap food for a long time and we have not been paying the real price for what we eat because the environmental cost has never been factored into our grocery bills. Now climate change has come along and forced the question upon us: can we continue to eat this way?

·

The effects of the changing climate are already being felt on the Prairies. A report published in 2007 by Natural Resources Canada and Environment Canada that examines the effects of climate change in this country notes that in Alberta, spring is starting twenty-six days earlier than it did a hundred years ago. Across the Prairies, the water levels during the summer are lower than before because there's not as much snow cover in the mountains and the summer runoff doesn't fill the rivers and lakes like it used to. These changes are consistent with the scientific models that predict that in this part of the world, temperatures will rise, rain patterns will shift and droughts will be more prevalent.

"We can expect conditions that are wetter and drier than we've ever experienced since Europeans came to Western Canada, since the 1880s," explained David Sauchyn, a senior research scientist with the Prairie Adaptation Research Collaborative who is part of a team assessing the potential influence of climate change on the Prairies and investigating adaptation requirements for communities. They are studying the climate of the past one thousand years by examining tree-ring records to provide context for hypothesizing about future change. "All the models indicate that it's getting warmer," said Sauchyn. "There isn't a single model that suggests cooler conditions. That's the most certain condition we have."

Most of the warming, as well as an increase in precipitation, is predicted to take place in the winter; the scientists also believe summers will become more intense. "The best scientific information indicates quite a bit warmer winters and springs, but summer will be dryer, longer and warmer," Sauchyn said. "This isn't good for agriculture." This means that as the median temperature increases and the Prairies lose their cold winters, more pests and diseases will be able to survive from one year to the next. Severe droughts are also extremely likely.

We only have to look back to the 1930s to see how droughts, insects and unpredictable weather patterns affect farming. Back then, while the rest of the world was experiencing the devastating effects of the Great Depression, the farmers who had made their homes in Palliser's Triangle, a semi-arid zone that straddles Saskatchewan and Alberta, were experiencing an even more profound crisis on top of the economic one. A turbulent climate had disturbed the delicate balance these farmers shared with the land. A multi-year drought hit the area, and the soil that had yielded the farmers bushels of wheat turned into dust that blew around like snow. Journalist James H. Gray described the conditions in his book *Men Against the Desert:* "The drifts built up till they covered fences, choked out the shelter belts and gardens, reached the roofs of the chicken houses, blew in through the cracks around farmhouse windows and under farmhouse doors to drive inhabitants out of their houses and out of the country."

The desert that started in 1929 grew a little bigger each year, eventually affecting what is estimated to be 18 million acres—the equivalent of a quarter of Canada's arable land. Then, in 1933, just when it seemed that the struggling farmers might finally harvest a good crop, the grasshoppers descended. Two years later, the crop was attacked by rust, and the next year, in 1936, the summer's heat broke records. Then there were other insects, varieties of sawflies and caterpillars that had never been seen before in Canada but had blown in on the winds. Between the drought, the heat and the insect invasions, this was a brutal time. When the Red Cross launched an appeal for the destitute of the region, there were 125,000 farm families on their list.

"The thirties showed that you can have periods of drought which extend over a number of years and that the existing capacity of the system to deal with drought is exceeded," said Barry Smit, a geography professor at the University of Guelph and the Canada research chair in global environmental change. "Lots of people lost their farms, they lost their livelihoods, the soil was ruined. The lesson from the thirties is that when you get a series of droughts, it may exceed our coping mechanisms." The way we grow food today will have to adapt to a new climate, he said, just as it needs to respond to changes in the market and advances in technology.

Climate change might force an answer to the question of how we can feed ourselves into the future *and* live sustainably. A growing group on the Prairies believe that they've already found that answer.

·

Keith Neu is not the only farmer in Saskatchewan who has abandoned the conventional path and switched to organics. While the numbers of organic farmers remain in the minority on the Prairies, enough farmers are tossing out the chemicals to call this trickle towards sustainable farming a movement. Across the Prairies, the number of organic farms is on the rise, particularly in Saskatchewan. In 1992, there were 190 certified organic farms in that province. This number grew to 1,230 by 2005. Provincial governments across the region have hired organics specialists to help farmers convert their operations, and the Government of Manitoba has even created a fund to cover the costs of organic certification—about $1,000.

The reasons for the switch vary from farm to farm. Some farmers say they went organic because they saw their neighbour making a little more money—they get paid a substantial premium on organic wheat. In some families, it is the woman on the farm who decides she doesn't want the kids exposed to the chemicals anymore—if the wind is blowing a certain way, I was told, you can taste the pesticides in the air on a spraying day. At least two men who now farm organically explained to me that they switched because they were getting sick from the chemicals they handled. Another, a potato farmer, joked that he could have killed an entire town with all the chemicals he was using. But some say the biggest push factor towards more holistic methods of working their soil is the prohibitive price of chemical fertilizers and pesticides. Farms in Saskatchewan spent about $965 million on fertilizers in 2007. When farmers convert their farms from conventional to organic, it's not just about getting rid of the chemicals. There is a fundamental difference in how the organic farmer views the soil. Organic farmers have what could be argued to be a complex relationship with their land. Whereas the conventional farmer can boost the soil's fertility in one afternoon with a dose of commercial fertilizer, an organic farmer must understand the soil and know what it needs to thrive over a long period. This means the organic farmer has to cultivate not only crops but a relationship with the land. It's a relationship where the farmer plays the role of doting caregiver, tending to the needs of the soil, offering everything required to make it stronger.

Organic farmers draw on skills developed through millennia of farming. To maintain the soil's health, farmers mulch the earth, spreading vegetable matter to prevent erosion as well as to help retain water. They use manure to restore and build the nutrients in the soil. They rotate crops from year to year, so one type of plant doesn't deplete the soil of a certain nutrient, and then use cover crops that fix nitrogen in the earth for next season's plants to use. Then there's the rest of the ecosystem, which plays a role in organic agriculture too. The insects that pollinate, the spiders that keep these insects in check, the birds that eat the spiders, the trees and grasses and flowers that provide habitat. Everything is unified in one indivisible system. If this wasn't nature at work, it would be magic.

We've recently learned that organic agriculture is better for climate change. Organic agriculture provides society with environmental goods and services. In addition to growing foods, organic fields perform a number of other jobs. For starters, agricultural soils actually act as carbon sinks. Plants like grasses and so-called weeds sequester carbon by taking carbon dioxide out of the atmosphere and storing it in their roots. Since organic soil is healthier than soil that has been treated with chemicals, it has more fibre, retains water better and doesn't erode as easily—erosion also releases carbon into the air. A Food and Agriculture Organization report on organics and climate change noted that "the carbon sink idea of the Kyoto Protocol may therefore partly be accomplished efficiently by organic agriculture." All agriculture can remove carbon dioxide from the atmosphere this way, but organic agriculture apparently does it more efficiently. In Europe, greenhouse gas emissions have been calculated to be 48 to 66 percent lower per hectare in organic farming systems.[13]

Similar results have been found in North America. The Rodale Institute, a non-profit research institute in Pennsylvania, has been conducting the longest-running North American study comparing conventional farming techniques with organic ones. Its study concludes that organic soils can mitigate climate change. It found that after twenty-seven years, organic soils had a 30 percent increase in carbon levels as opposed to the conventional soil, which some studies have shown actually loses carbon to the atmosphere. The institute advocates for what it calls regenerative organic farming that would improve the soils for future generations as well as help to lower the amount of carbon in our atmosphere.

Some studies have found that organic yields are not as high as those on industrial farms—though other studies, such as one out of the University of Michigan in 2007, have found the opposite, in fact showing that organic agriculture in the developing world produced *more* food than conventional farming. Given the pressure of climate change, can we afford *not* to turn to organics?

. . .

If farmers were afforded the same kind of celebrity status as actors or athletes, Marc Loiselle would be the Al Pacino of farming. He has been around, has done his time and has accomplished some great things—he's a star farmer, or "starmer." Chefs and bakers across Canada know that Marc is the man behind Red Fife wheat, and he has won recognition from people around the world for his work to reintroduce the heritage wheat listed in Slow Food International's Ark of Taste. But it has been a long journey to this place.

Marc is a grain farmer from Vonda, Saskatchewan, population 322. It is a small town not unlike others on the Prairies. There's a school for the local kids and a co-op where the farmers can buy fuel and hardware and not much else. There used to be a CN Rail station when Marc started to work on his family farm in 1971, but that has closed down. The grain elevators were demolished when CN centralized its grain pickups. The old wooden platform at the station where the farmers used to bring their milk cans brimming with the morning's cream was destroyed around the same time. Also gone are the town's bakery and cheese store, just like in most other small Prairie towns, now that people drive to shop.

It's all testimony to how life has changed on the Prairies and how farming is no longer sustaining vibrant communities. For kilometres around Vonda, you will see farm after farm growing acres of cash crops. Marc Loiselle's own farm isn't far from Vonda, in a valley that is an ancient glacial lake. Half of the 960 acres they own is up on what would have been the shore of the lake. The earth there is glacial till, gravelly and not ideal planting soil. But down on what was the lake bed, the earth is black and rich. This is where he grows his organic Red Fife wheat.

You wouldn't really know that the Loiselle family farm is any different from its neighbours—although the twenty thousand trees they've planted around the place as a windbreak to prevent erosion could be your first hint that Marc does things differently than most. He's been farming his ancestors' land since he got married and his parents moved into town so he could become the primary farmer. Today, he sows close to eight hundred acres of organic crops, a third of it wheat, the rest flax, oats, barley, mustard and a fall rye.

Marc Loiselle inadvertently fell into Red Fife, not knowing that he was launching a revival. It all began back in 2001, when a seed-saver friend grew some old Red Fife in pots. This friend had received the seeds from a woman in British Columbia who had been working with heritage seeds, trying to grow some grain varieties that hadn't been planted in decades. Marc's friend would turn up at meetings of the local organic farming chapter with a gallon pail of wheat, trying to entice people to grow the crop. At first Marc wasn't interested. Then someone he knew took some of the wheat and grew an entire field—an important turn of events because in one season, this man built up the local supply of seed. When he offered Marc a third of the harvest for a good price, Marc sowed it that fall, and his relationship with Red Fife began.

Red Fife is probably the most famous strain of wheat available today in Canada. Articles have been written about it and chefs expound on its enticing qualities—the chewiness of its crumb, the way it bakes into a deep, golden colour, the flavour of its bran that offers a depth and a nuttiness. While conventional flour is white and almost powdery, Red Fife is red, its bran tinting the flour, and it is almost sandy in texture. I've taken to using it when I cook, and it makes dense yet moist muffins and quick breads and the best waffles I've ever eaten. Foods baked with regular flour taste like cardboard when compared with those made with Red Fife.

This heirloom strain of wheat is an early predecessor, a genetic grandparent, to what you find in a sack of flour today. Back in the 1800s, Red Fife was grown by just about every wheat farmer in Canada. On farms in Ontario before the turn of the twentieth century, they would have sown Red Fife in the spring. It is a landrace, a species that adapts to its environment, and so the wheat tailored itself to the conditions of North America and did well under the pressures of climate and disease. In fact, in large part because of Red Fife, Europeans were able to settle the prairies, transforming the grasslands into a wheat-producing region. The plant matured a little earlier than the other varieties people were growing, and that suited the climate in the West. The farmers were able to harvest their wheat before the frost, which made it possible for the settlers to stay.

Red Fife wheat came to Canada possibly via Scotland. The exact route is not known, but one version of the story holds that a Scottish farmer named David Fife, living in Upper Canada, was given some seeds by a friend in Glasgow who had collected them from a Polish ship loaded with Ukrainian wheat. David and his wife, Jane, planted this wheat on their farm near Peterborough in 1842. While most of the wheat didn't do well, there was one plant stalk that grew much taller than the rest. So David Fife decided to plant the seed kernels from that one head of wheat, and slowly, over a period of a few years, built up his store of seeds. He found that the wheat he was growing did very well in the Ontario climate and, as the story goes, was impressed by the flavour of the grain.

Soon Red Fife became the grain of choice and remained dominant until it was replaced in the early twentieth century by a new, hardier strain that matured even earlier called Marquis, which was bred by mixing Red Fife with Hard Red Calcutta from India. Quickly, Red Fife disappeared. Throughout the decades that followed, other varieties of wheat were bred, and virtually any Canadian wheat grown in the Prairies today includes Red Fife as part of its genetic ancestry.

Marc is the country's top supplier of Red Fife. He sells his grains to bakeries all over Canada as well as to other farmers who grow it but still can't meet the high demand for the flour where they live. It's so popular in Ontario that some farmers who are unable to grow enough buy Marc's wheat, which they mill themselves and then resell. "Red Fife is the best variety of grain," said Marc. "If you judge it for taste and baking quality, all those years of grain development weren't worth it."

•

It is unlikely that the Red Fife renaissance would have taken place had someone not saved its seeds decades ago. When the last fields of Red Fife were being harvested and then replaced with modern strains, farmers' access to the seeds would have disappeared completely had someone not had the foresight—or the nostalgia—to hang on to some of the grain. In Canada, the government often performs this task, and seed vaults preserve the genes of our food in a handful of locations across the country. These days, seed saving, the age-old practice of collecting the best seeds from your plants to grow in succeeding years, is rising in popularity in Canada and around the world. People have saved their seeds since humans first started to grow food; however, it took the commercialization of the seed industry to make preserving them an almost political act. The seed-saving movement began in the 1960s, when gardeners started to notice that the plants they were accustomed to growing from year to year were no longer sold by the seed companies. In an act of self-preservation, people started to collect their seeds and formed groups to help spread the knowledge about how to do this right.

At the helm of the seed-saving movement in Canada is an organization called Seeds of Diversity. It's a small group, run out of a tiny office in Waterloo, Ontario, and it subsists on a patchwork of grants and membership fees as well as sales of its publications. The group was started in 1984 by a handful of organic gardeners who wanted to take control of their seed stock. The mandate they set still survives and is supported by people across the country. Seeds of Diversity runs a number of programs, such as the Great Canadian Garlic Collection, in which gardeners all over Canada keep over a hundred varieties of garlic in existence by planting them each year in their gardens. The group is also tracking the state of the nation's pollinators, as their ultimate goal is to preserve the biodiversity of our food supply.

Seeds are part of the global food chain and have been subjected to the same homogenizing forces as tomatoes and beef cattle. These days, seeds are produced like fast-food hamburgers. In various countries, specifically in Asia and in South America but also in Israel and the United States too, vast farms specialize in seed production, growing most of the seeds for vegetables and fruits that are planted around the world, not just for people's home gardens but for farms as well. Bob Wildfong is the executive director of Seeds of Diversity and a horticulturalist. "Let's take the pepper seed," he said, explaining how the big farms provide the same seed stock to many different seed catalogues. "You might have one farm that grows just peppers. They would take all the peppers and crush them and let them sit for a few days to let the seeds separate from the pulp. Then they'd collect hundreds of thousands of pounds of pepper seeds. You could then pick up five different seed catalogues and be able to find the same pepper seeds from the same farm."

These seeds are then grown by gardeners in Toronto, Miami, Vancouver, and all sorts of places with extremely different climates. However, the pepper seeds that were grown in South America would be best adapted to tropical conditions and therefore not suited to Canada—or wherever else in the world they end up. And everywhere, the peppers would be the same—the same variety with the same taste. You would similarly find seeds from plants adapted to a different climate if you purchased seed corn imported from South America, or onion seeds that are on display in the racks at the grocery store that likely originate in Israel, or the so-called Canadian seed potatoes that are produced in Cuba to sell to farmers back home.

Seed saving is important, said Bob Wildfong, because by retaining the genetic material of plants and sowing them every year in our gardens, we preserve the diversity of our food supply. In fact, the future of our food depends on it. The entire security of our food system is dependent on being able to breed new varieties of food-producing plants by crossing genes from the older strains. Plant breeders in the future, for example, could turn to heritage strains of wheat to create a new wheat for the Prairies better suited to new weather patterns. "I view the heritage-plant gene pool as a large part of the biodiversity of our food system," said Wildfong. "What we have here isn't just a historical curiosity. What we have here is 95 percent of our plant gene pool. Whether it is change that is forced on us like climate change or declining fossil fuels, these things are going to change the plants we can grow. The whole food system is going to operate differently. To have plants that can adapt to climate change so we can grow more food, we have to dip back into the plant gene pool."

And herein lies the significance of Red Fife wheat. While the grain itself may not be the answer to sustainable agriculture in Canada and might never take over from whatever hybrid is milled and packaged in the bag of flour at the grocery store today, this heritage variety is a symbol of possibility. It demonstrates that old grains might come in handy in the future, that there's a benefit to keeping these things around. Right now Red Fife offers an economic and taste advantage. But who knows what it, or other varieties of wheat, might contribute to in the future. It is easy to undervalue those small, insignificant-looking seeds. But really, we can't survive without them. The way that Marc Loiselle produces Red Fife on his organic farm demonstrates that a new way of farming grain is possible on the Prairies, and elsewhere.

Now Marc is experimenting with more heritage grains. He has planted two winter wheats that he finds intriguing, one from Germany and Rouge de Bordeaux from France. These just might be the next Red Fife.

Certainly, Marc's creative thinking about farming, this dreaming up of new ideas and ways of looking at the food we eat and the ways we produce it, is what we need to push agriculture to the next level and create a sustainable food system in Canada. And while Marc is thinking out of the box, others are using their ingenuity to build boxes—and grow our food.

CHAPTER FOUR

THE FOUR-SEASON FARM

A Sustainable Winter Harvest in Ontario

The kale seeds had been planted only twelve hours before and already they were coming to life. A tiny shoot no wider than a pin was beginning to uncurl, the earliest sign of the cotyledon, a seed's first leaves that push through the casing after germination. About a tablespoon's worth of these now budding seeds were heaped on the top of a small plug that looked like an oversized cork made of soil. It was in this plug that, in the coming days, the kale seeds would set roots and grow into a plant with leaves about six inches tall, the perfect size for a baby-leaf salad mix. This particular plug was lined up with seventy-four others in a black heat-absorbing tray, moist and humid to simulate the perfect conditions for germination in a summer garden bed. The beginning of new life is an awesome sight.

Jo Slegers stared at his seeds intently, as if he too was amazed at witnessing the start of the miracle that is photosynthesis, a plant's ability to use the sun's electromagnetic radiation to turn the carbon dioxide in the air into plant tissue we can see, touch and dress with a vinaigrette to enjoy for lunch. He picked up one of the plugs and brought it close to his face, examining the seeds with the same open expression of wonder that I often see in my daughters when I show them something in nature that is new to them. He then placed the lid gently back on the tray and looked around his greenhouse at rows and rows of leafy green plants in various stages of growth—more kale, lettuce, tatsoi, mustards—and up at the sun that was beating down at that moment, shining through the roof made of plastic sheeting.

"It's hot in here," I said to Jo. He nodded when I stated the obvious; he is acutely aware of the conditions in the greenhouse at all times. Jo is constantly monitoring the light levels in the greenhouses, furrowing his brow when a cloud covers the sun or ensuring the ventilation system activates when the sun's rays have overheated the place. At that moment, with the sun free of clouds, I was sweating and uncomfortable in the heat, and it was hard to believe that it was mid-December on the other side of the plastic, with the day's forecasted high of minus six degrees. Snow and ice covered the fields outside, and the boughs of the evergreens by Jo's house were white with snow. As I started to take off my coat, Jo motioned to the walls of the greenhouse. He pointed to the vents that span the entire length of the building. He was so in tune with the functioning of the greenhouse that moments before the computer monitoring the conditions inside opened these vents to let in fresh air and a new supply of carbon dioxide for the plants to breathe, he warned me that they were about to do this. Within seconds, fresh cold air spilled into the space. The plants and I were happy.

Jo Slegers is a farmer in Middlesex County, Ontario, who specializes in organic edible greens—salad greens and herbs such as basil and cilantro and all sorts of sprouts. He cultivates these plants inside his greenhouses year-round, using soil plugs that are nourished by a hydroponic system. The buildings cover just over half an acre, which means when I visited, there were about forty thousand leafy green plants growing at one time that would become fresh, local salad in the coming days. Inside the greenhouse, there was the constant sound of water flowing through the dozens of rows of white plastic troughs, raised on narrow legs to waist level, that stretch from one end of the building to the other. It looked like a floating green carpet. Plugs sprouting plants started a few weeks before the kale seeds we had just examined sat in little holes in these troughs, where they received a continuous supply of water mixed with a liquid compost fertilizer. Above the troughs, suspended from the roof of the greenhouse, were growth-inducing lights, ceramic halides that mimic over 90 percent of the sun's spectrum of rays, as well as a ventilation system that kept the temperature at 18 degrees Celsius. All this equipment is protected not by glass walls but by very expensive plastic sheeting from Italy—about $150,000 worth altogether—which traps the sunshine and insulates the structure. In this human-made environment, I felt very distant from the farmers' fields I had stood in at harvest time only a few weeks earlier.

But unlike the field crops that came out of the ground in the fall, this operation feeds people year round. Slegers Greens, Jo's company, supplies about 55,000 boxes of produce a year to restaurants and grocers mostly in Southern Ontario (a small amount is exported to the United States and Quebec through a wholesaler). Jo is forty-three years old, with a boyish face, freckles, tousled hair and a casual manner that gives you the impression that he approaches life much like a kid does, with a curious wonder. As he led me through his greenhouses, he pointed out the plants he finds interesting, such as the red amaranth, which is so bright it looks neither natural nor edible. "Take a look at this," he said, motioning to the technicolor leaves. When I asked him about the technology he uses, he was humble. "I think you could keep it under the mom-and-pop category," he said. "It's very crude, this stuff here." He understands the value of messing around as a way of trying to figure out new methods of growing. "Most things we learn are because someone got sloppy with something." He pointed to a tray of recently planted spinach seeds that were covered in vermiculite, a thin, flaking rock that he uses as a growing medium for some of his plants; he's found that the vermiculite prevents the spinach from moulding. "One day, the vermiculite spilled onto half a tray, but then that half did better than the rest." Now they sprinkle it on all the spinach seeds. Later, when he explained the irrigation system, his face lit up as he picked up a piece of tubing that had a hot pink plastic toggle stuck in the end. "This is Lite-Brite!" he said excitedly. "We needed something to plug the tubing up so we grabbed whatever crap we had in the house." It's easy to understand how a guy like him got into an unconventional type of farming.

Slegers has been growing lettuce in the greenhouse since 1987, when he was only twenty-one and wanted to do something different on his family's tobacco farm. This farm was a small operation, and as a kid, Jo had helped with everything from the planting to the curing in their drying houses. But when it came time for him to decide what he would do with his life, he knew there wasn't a future in tobacco. At a community meeting one day, an older farmer who grew Boston lettuce in his greenhouse asked the crowd if anyone there was interested in doing something new, something innovative. Jo put up his hand. Within seven months, he and his dad had built a greenhouse on their property, and Jo started to grow Boston lettuce that he sold to local grocers. Two years later, they built a second greenhouse and then a third. Today, his business employs eleven local people, and both he and his wife, Pauline, work on the farm too. They received organic certification in December 2004 and sell their specialty greens to chefs and upscale grocers.

Standing in Jo's greenhouse, amid the kale and the mustards, I wondered if this controlled environment could be the way to guarantee a steady and local supply of fresh greens and other summer vegetables all winter long. Eating locally is easy to do in the summer, when the bounty of the region is readily available at farmers' markets. Towards the end of the growing season's parade of vegetables—asparagus, then peas, beans, new potatoes, zucchini, squash, tomatoes—it's easy to believe that a local food economy could feed us the variety we've grown accustomed to eating year-round. But by March, when many of the foods from around here that had been in storage start to run out and the first crops are still many weeks away, it's more difficult to eat locally and maintain that variety and freshness we now take for granted. When winter is well under way, I start to look enviously at those California greens stacked in the grocery store. When I'm making dinner with a sprouting rutabaga from my root vegetable basket, the imported collard greens at the supermarket that are old and leathery look positively spring-like and enticing.

So are greenhouses the missing piece in this puzzle? Are they the answer to getting us from October to May? Could greenhouses be a way to entice everybody—and I mean everybody, not just those committed to reducing their food miles at all cost—to buy local? Is a strong greenhouse industry what we need to build a sustainable foodshed in Canada?

．

Greenhouses in Canada are big business. We are the largest producer of greenhouse tomatoes in this hemisphere. In the Fraser Valley, in Quebec and near Medicine Hat and Red Cliff, Alberta, greenhouses grow mostly tomatoes, cucumbers and peppers for a good part of the year. But it's in Southern Ontario where this kind of agriculture has really flourished. There are more than two thousand acres of greenhouses in Niagara and Essex counties alone. Essex has the largest concentration of greenhouses in North America, with 87 percent of operations dedicated to vegetable production. The number of greenhouses in the area has been rising since the early 1990s; between 1992 and 2002, production of greenhouse tomatoes alone grew more than 600 percent. One reason for this expansion is the American consumer's desire for different varieties of tomatoes (like those grape cherry tomatoes packed in plastic clamshells that have become ubiquitous at the supermarket in the past few years). These varieties are developed much more quickly in a greenhouse.

To meet the demand, these all-season farms housing the tomato vines have become really big: the largest greenhouse vegetable grower in the Leamington, Ontario, area farms a whopping fifty-one acres of controlled-environment beds. Inside these climatically stable bubbles, slender tomato vines rise as much as ten metres; delicate stalks of cucumber plants are suspended by string to allow the fruit to hang evenly in the light; and pepper blossoms bask in the grow lights. Bumblebees, kept in cardboard hives, buzz about, fertilizing the plants, and parasitic wasps keep aphids in check. Inside it's a veritable mini ecosystem, impervious to the hazards of Mother Nature. There are so many greenhouses in Essex with their ever-shining grow lights that on a clear night people say they cast an eerie glow over the land.

The United States is the primary destination for Essex County's vegetables. Tomatoes, and to a lesser extent cucumbers and peppers, are shipped across the continent, with annual export sales from Ontario's greenhouses hovering around the $700-million mark. But while sales figures may be high, the profits aren't necessarily great, because of the steep costs in know-how, technology and capital required to run such an operation. To operate a greenhouse, you must first understand horticulture. You need to be able to navigate the technology, like computer programs that regulate temperature, irrigation and fertilization. And to start out, you'll need a significant amount of money. According to Gene Giacomelli, a professor of agriculture and biosystems engineering and the director of the Controlled Environment Agriculture Center at the University of Arizona, an average-sized greenhouse will set you back $630,000. This price includes the structure, the equipment, the heating system and anything else needed to start growing food. And then, of course, there's the cost of the land.

I was nevertheless surprised to discover that greenhouse production in Canada is extremely secretive. While researching this book, I found that people consistently didn't return my calls or reply to my email messages. One of the groups representing Ontario greenhouse grow-ers wouldn't disclose the names of greenhouse operators, citing privacy concerns, and when I did get a greenhouse researcher who works for the Ontario government on the phone, he would only speak to me off the record, in hushed tones. An American academic who has been studying greenhouses for decades confided to me that growers who call her up for advice don't even tell her the details of their production. In the words of another academic, they fear "spilling the beans." I quickly got the sense that there is an arms race of sorts between the growers, a competition to try to find the perfect way to produce tomatoes in the off-season and make a buck. And really, when I think about it in these terms, it is the ultimate struggle against nature's rhythms. To overcome the constraints of the Canadian seasons, to transform December into June, dormancy into fertility, using grow lights, computers, fertilizers and a little bit of luck, is a feat as incredible as sending a human to the moon.

Despite the modern Canadian greenhouse industry's reliance on tech-nology, these glass houses, as they have been called through the ages, were invented centuries ago. Humans have long wanted to grow their favourite plants out of season, to find a way to keep tropical trees thriving all year round outside their native climatic zone. The earliest known attempts at growing under glass took place in Roman times, when gardeners tried to force plants to blossom and fruit earlier than they would naturally by building hotbeds, which are planting beds filled with manure, a substance that gives off heat for months, to warm the roots of the plants. While the Romans did know how to make glass, they weren't able to produce a flat pane that was clear enough to allow sunlight to pass through, so they placed sheets of mica over these hotbeds. They were thus able to grow frost-sensitive crops such as cucumbers and melons in cooler months. In the ruins of Pompeii, archaeologists found an early greenhouse: a struc-ture with a mica wall, a heating system and masonry shelves for potted plants. But it wasn't until a French gardening expert named Olivier de

Serres, in a bid to find a way to house orange trees all year round in Europe, published a book describing his plans for a thatched-roof house with glass walls and skylights that the modern construction of a greenhouse began to take shape. (The French word for greenhouse, *serre*, is testimony to this man's contribution.)

Whereas the early greenhouses were primarily used for citrus trees, by the 1900s, greenhouses contributed to food systems both in Europe and North America. A greenhouse industry developed towards the end of the nineteenth century, primarily in northwestern Europe, to satisfy the demand for early-season fruits and vegetables. In North America, greenhouses were run by Dutch, Italian and Portuguese immigrants who transplanted their growing tradition to their new environment. In Leamington, the centre of Canada's greenhouse-tomato industry today, these European immigrants continued to farm the vegetables they were familiar with.

After the war, however, the food system started to industrialize. California emerged as a powerful exporter of fresh produce, and the smaller family-owned greenhouses had a hard time competing with the vegetables trucked in from warmer climates far away. The next generation of greenhouse growers had no incentive to invest in the ageing infrastructure their parents had built, and many closed down. In Leamington, however, the industry continued to thrive and became one of the largest greenhouse centres on the continent.

·

Jo Slegers's greenhouses—just like the greenhouses of ancient Greece, just like the greenhouses of nineteenth-century Europe and Leamington—are designed to create the optimal conditions for plant growth. With their transparent walls and roofs, greenhouses maximize the amount of light, or solar radiation, while maintaining a steady temperature indoors. With the help of modern technology, they keep humidity low and carbon dioxide levels high to stimulate plant growth. The greenhouses feature mechanical systems that maintain air circulation because just one chilly air pocket can slow plant growth. And roots, like leaves, have their own requirements. Greenhouse growers provide ready access to water, nutrients and dissolved oxygen.

As long as you give a plant everything it needs to survive, you can grow anything inside a greenhouse, in any environment. Greenhouses have been built in the most hostile climates, including the deserts of Iran and Abu Dhabi as well as in hot and dry American states such as Arizona and California. There is even a greenhouse at the South Pole, housed in an American research station built on a 3,000-metre-thick sheet of moving ice. Despite the average outdoor temperature of minus 49 degrees Celsius, lettuce and even strawberries are grown to feed the researchers who live at the station. The research project is run by the Controlled Environment Agriculture Center in preparation for a future greenhouse on Mars.

After Jo's kale seeds sprout, the plug is moved to the long troughs that stretch the width of the greenhouse, where the plants will reach maturity. There, the roots will drink from a stream of fertilizer-rich water. The leaves will bask in the sun, which, in the shorter growing days of winter, will be supplemented by the high-spectrum bulbs. It pays to supplement the light source, even though Jo must pay for the hydro, because from November through February, when light levels are low, for every 1 percent increase in sunlight, there is a 1 percent increase in the plant's green tissue production. While Jo can continue to grow greens throughout the winter, Ontario's tomato and pepper growers cease their operations for December and January. In their case, it costs too much money to crank up the lights to compensate for the waning sun.

Hydroponic greenhouses like Jo's produce astoundingly high yields. One acre of hydroponic greenhouse can produce an astronomical 600,000 pounds of food per acre per year, whereas a one-acre field will produce 90 percent *less*. This is because, of course, a field produces only one crop in the summer, whereas the greenhouse operates at least ten months of the year. What also boosts production is that a farmer can deliver fertilizer directly to the roots, unlike in a field, where the roots take up only what they can access, and unused fertilizer seeps into the soil or runoff and pollutes groundwater.

Even though you can grow anything in a greenhouse, deciding what to plant, and when, requires weighing the costs of production with the benefits of growing. But greenhouses don't have to be large enterprises to grow food. The technology is flexible. A greenhouse can be as simple as a homemade cold frame to protect crops from frost to a more expensive plastic-sheeting tunnel that isn't heated or vented but shelters plants and is big enough for a tractor to pass through. There are all types of greenhouses on farms across the country—in fact, most of the farms I visited used some form of a cold frame to start their seedlings long before the frosts had passed or to extend the harvest well into the fall. And while the optimal conditions for greenhouses exist only in limited areas of Canada—moderate temperature extremes and abundant sunlight—greenhouses can be found in the most unexpected of places, such as the Queen Charlotte Islands. On one of the small islands, a man named George Pattison harvests tomatoes and cucumbers from May to October in his own greenhouses.

Pattison calls the rugged beach and the coastal forest where he lives and farms Fantasy Island, which isn't surprising, as it really is a fantasy to grow these fresh foods hydroponically, despite the lack of light during a good part of the year due to its northerly latitude. George starts his tomato plants in November, when the weather in the Queen Charlottes is windy and stormy and it is dark for much of the day. In December there can be as many as seventeen hours of darkness in a twenty-four-hour period, for which he must compensate with lights. And yet, the Fantasy Island farm is able to coax out of these conditions a healthy supply of produce—from George's nine hundred tomato plants he gets about 450 kilograms of fruit, and his fifty-four cucumbers provide him with 14 kilograms a day—which he sells at the local farmers' market and a few grocery stores. His achievements demonstrate that a greenhouse can supplement the local food supply just about anywhere in Canada. However, for a local food system to be sustainable, one must assess how much energy a greenhouse requires.

.

The question of what makes one greenhouse more efficient than another comes down to energy used per unit of food produced. Grow lights require some energy, but most of a greenhouse's demand is for heat. In the Netherlands, a country with a large greenhouse industry, academics have contemplated the question of what makes a sustainable greenhouse. Erik van Os, a scientist at the research institute Wageningen UR Greenhouse Horticulture who has been studying soilless growing systems for more than two decades, is currently working on reducing nutrient and pesticide emissions in hydroponic systems. He told me that hydroponics have a better ratio of energy input to food output because their yields per square metre are higher than growing in soil; also, these systems discharge fewer pesticides and fertilizers into the sewage system or surface water. Although greenhouses in warmer countries such as Spain may use less energy to grow food, a greenhouse in a colder climate such as the Netherlands can use technology to level the differences. For example, northern green-houses can harvest heat in the summer and save it to be used in the future, thus reducing their carbon footprint. In the Netherlands, for example, van Os explained that the summer heat is harvested in the day and stored in insulated tanks to be used at night; heat can also be stored long-term in underground aquifers. To reduce the amount of energy greenhouses require, thermal screens can be used to cover the roof, minimizing heat loss at night. Operators could also generate their own electricity, or take advantage of innovations such as geothermal heating systems. While the southern greenhouses have the advantage of a longer growing season, the northern growers have technology on their side. "I don't think there will be much difference in sustainability between a northern and a southern tomato," van Os concluded.

In Canada, too, scientists are considering how greenhouses can produce the best food for the least cost, both environmental and financial. David Ehret, a scientist at the federally funded Pacific Agri-Food Research Centre, in British Columbia, studies this issue. He has investigated the nutritional content of greenhouse vegetables and has developed blueberry and raspberry plants that will produce fruit in the winter to satisfy Canadians' year-round craving for berries. From the passion in Ehret's voice, it's easy to tell he is a huge proponent of greenhouse production. "It's amazing what can be done in a greenhouse," he said with excitement. He believes this kind of agriculture could play an important role in a sustainable local foodshed. "If the urban population wants it enough, there's got to be ways to make it happen. But in order to do that, there are a lot of inputs. The greenhouse has to be heated throughout the winter. There is a big labour component because something has to be done every day. The fruit has to be picked, the vines need to be wound around a string. The structure itself is very expensive," he said. "If we had a million more greenhouses than we do now, we would probably feed the planet. But at what cost?"

The cost could in fact be high. Because plants use carbon dioxide in photosynthesis, some greenhouse operations burn fuel for the sole purpose of producing carbon dioxide to pump into their buildings to stimulate plant growth. Many operators who burn fuel to heat their greenhouses in the colder months—and use the by-product carbon dioxide to stimulate growth—continue to fabricate carbon dioxide in the summer even though they don't need the heat. Considering that carbon dioxide is one of the greenhouse gases that we're trying to reduce, the ecological footprint of such an operation is massive. When the price of natural gas shot up in the fall of 2008, it was reported that some greenhouses in the Leamington area switched to coal as their source of heat—not exactly environmentally friendly.

However, David Ehret remains hopeful that sustainable practices will prevail. Because greenhouse production is such an expensive form of agriculture, operators are always looking for ways to reduce their input costs, and as a result are often making environmentally positive decisions because they are forced to. "They really do push the limits," he said. "Because they are so technically advanced, they are pushed to solve problems." For example, twenty-five years ago, operators were letting excess fertilizer drain away as effluent; now they collect it and pump it back through the cycle so there is less polluting waste. Many operators are also employing environmentally sensitive techniques, such as using green power or capturing rainwater to meet all their irrigation needs and minimize their burden on the local water table. They are also applying integrated pest management, or IPM, a pest control program for farmers that aims to eliminate the use of pesticides by using prevention, observation and intervention instead of regular spraying. These types of innovations make greenhouses a positive addition to a local and sustainable food chain, said Ehret.

Mike Schreiner calls himself a social entrepreneur. He is the former vice-president of Local Food Plus, a non-profit organization that is trying to build a sustainable food system for Toronto, and he has been the leader of the Green Party of Ontario since November 2009. Throughout his career, he has thought a lot about how to foster a sustainable, regional food system. In 1996, he started the first commercial organic food box program in the city. He sees greenhouses as a sustainable way to provide variety for the Canadian diet during the winter. "We have the technology and the capacity to operate greenhouses in environmentally friendly ways. Now, whether the marketplace allows us to do it on a cost basis is to be seen," he said. "One of the problems is that we don't internalize the costs of externalities in the system. If we paid the true cost of what it takes to ship broccoli from California to Toronto, that economic equation would change."

In April 2009, it cost US$2 to ship an eight-pound flat of strawberries from California to Toronto in a special refrigerated truck with proper suspension to ensure a smooth ride. Flying raspberries from Chile cost two to three times that price. However, if the environmental cost of the truck's journey across the continent, or the plane's flight north, was factored into the shipping costs, then the fruit prices would rise substantially. That would provide an economic incentive to grow berries in greenhouses here in Canada. And these would be the first steps towards increasing off-season variety in our local produce.

■   ■   ■

When I first heard the term "farming on the back side of the calendar," I instantly loved the image it conjured up: a type of extreme farming for the courageous and daring. The concept involves growing your food outside in the winter, in a northern climate, and planted directly into the earth as opposed to hydroponically. Something about this approach feels wonderfully rebellious. What a tremendous challenge to focus your efforts on growing food in the earth outdoors, not in the summer, when the sun shines strongly, the air is warm and nature blooms, but in the winter, when the snow falls and the rest of the natural world falls dormant. When I say out-of-doors, I don't mean unprotected. When you farm on the back side of the calendar, you do use a rudimentary, often handmade, greenhouse to cover the plants, and inside this greenhouse, you supplement the protection of the plastic walls with what is called a sweater, a second layer of plastic, like a row cover, that is placed right on top of the plants to keep them a littler warmer. The secret to making this revolutionary technique work is in the plants you choose. Rather than traditional greenhouse species like tomatoes and cucumbers that rely on heat and artificial light in the winter, the off-season grower looks to green leaf plants like claytonia and mâche that have evolved to survive cold temperatures, even snow and frost.

Eliot Coleman coined the term "farming on the back side of the calendar." Since the 1970s, in the northeastern United States, he has developed his technique of turning winter ground into fertile soil and he has written three books on the topic. He began seriously experimenting with winter growing when he was managing a farm at a private school in Vermont that grew most of its own food and had integrated horticulture into its curriculum. Because the school year spans the winter months, students weren't involved in the vegetable growing that took place during summer holidays. Coleman thought that if they could help to grow the vegetables themselves, it would add to their education. So he started a winter gardening project to engage them in food production, and they experimented with different plants, particularly greens that thrived year-round in Europe. He quickly discovered that the prevailing belief that there isn't enough sunlight at his latitude to support growth from November through March was wrong. It wasn't a lack of light that was the problem but rather the cold temperatures. He found that if he adjusted the temperature, his greens thrived.

Coleman points out that if you look at the globe, you'll see that the eastern seaboard, where he lives, is at the same latitude as places in Europe where farmers are able to grow year-round. The hours of daylight are the same in both places, but in Europe, the Gulf Stream keeps winter temperatures warmer than it is at similar latitudes in North America. Heat-loving plants like tomatoes, squash and eggplant do not grow in Europe in the winter either, but some crops are harvested in those months. Coleman thought that if he could replicate Europe's winter growing conditions by keeping the plants at a similar temperature to Europe, then he could unlock a whole new growing season in the northern United States.

The results of his experiments were amazing. Once he figured out which plants to keep in the greenhouse, he was able to pick fresh food from his garden in January, even on the coldest days. He found that spinach, leeks and chard will tolerate outdoor temperatures as low as minus 30 degrees Celsius as long as they are protected. Mâche, green onions and tatsoi can even be picked when completely frozen. When they thaw, they look no different and make a great winter salad. Coleman planted carrots in August, about the time when traditional farmers harvest theirs. These carrots continued to grow into September in soil protected by a greenhouse. By the time he harvested them in the winter, they were a good size with a leafy green top. Inspired by his success, Coleman became even more creative; he discovered that baby salad leaves can freeze and thaw every night and still look good enough to eat. Over the next decade, Coleman tinkered some more, creating a planting schedule and inventing systems that improved his winter harvest. He said, "I kept on pushing the envelope, and finally we got rid of winter."

In 1990, he moved from the school back to his own farm. The winter growing had been so successful that he decided to start a winter vegetable-growing business to supply local restaurants with fresh greens and other vegetables picked while snow storms, hail and frigid temperatures raged outside. He and his wife, Barbara Damrosch, continue to run this business to this day and have done wonders for the local food economy. Throughout the year, they sell vegetables to nearby stores as well as to wholesalers and restaurants. And they do this without heating their greenhouses. This year-round growing has been financially successful too. The quarter-acre of greenhouses combined with the acre and a half of market garden Eliot and his wife cultivate in the summer garner them an income of $120,000 a year, with $65,000 being earned in the four summer months and $55,000 earned during the eight coldest months.

Good news: it's possible here in Canada too. North of Toronto, in Simcoe County, not far from where the housing developments of Vaughan taper into farmland, former chef turned farmer David Cohlmeyer is adapting Coleman's techniques to the Canadian winter. His farm, called Cookstown Greens, is down a gravel road that's covered with ice and snow when I make my way there in December. It's a modest-looking place with a couple of trailers, four greenhouses and a wooden building where the packing takes place. Cohlmeyer sends produce from his greenhouses to chefs at the city's most high-end restaurants. His staff sends out shipments of salad made up of thirty-five different greens and edible flowers, as well as root crops, leeks and other vegetables they grow outside in the summer months and store in their root cellar.

In the greenhouses, Cohlmeyer grows a mix of baby greens like sorrel, tatsoi and heritage mustards as well as coriander, fennel and edible flowers such as nasturtium and bachelor's buttons, which he harvests all year round. The greenhouses are covered by a simple peaked roof made from plastic sheeting over metal rods. Unlike Jo Slegers's hydroponics operation, he plants his crops directly in the earth. The greenhouse has a haphazard, almost cluttered feel about it. Growing boxes, pots and trays of sprouts are lined up on shelves. Along one side is a chest-high compost pile, where he cycles his earth. Cohlmeyer uses as little electricity and propane as possible. He has grow lights in only one of the greenhouses, and even in the coldest months the sun does most of the work of keeping the structures warm—though in the winter, the propane furnace kicks in, mostly at night, to make sure the temperature doesn't drop below zero. In the winter, the plants don't exactly burst forth with new growth, but Cohlmeyer is able to maintain his harvest in the darkest and coldest months. Come February, when the days become longer, the greenhouses warm up and plant growth quickens. Inside, on a sunny day, it can actually heat up so much he needs to open the vents.

Cohlmeyer's greens are well known as far as lettuce goes. The name of his farm appears on the menus of restaurants where they serve his produce. For the patron dining on winter tatsoi, it's a reminder that on the edge of the city, in a snowy back field not far from the 400 highway, a relatively simple greenhouse can produce fresh greens all year round.

. . .

A big problem for the local food economy in Canada is that we have grown accustomed to eating a lot more than Boston lettuce in January. I live a few blocks from Toronto's Chinatown East and I'm regularly amazed by the seemingly never-ending supply of tropical fruits and vegetables displayed outside these stores, despite deep-freeze temperatures, in crates bearing the names of far-flung places. There's durian, mangoes, bitter melon, Chinese broccoli, mushrooms of all sorts and long green vegetables that I cannot name. It's not just East Asian foods that are imported to Canada. Planes arrive at Pearson Airport regularly carrying guavas from Pakistan, a vegetable from India and Sri Lanka called a drumstick, curry leaves and green chilies from India. Our country's immigrant population has boosted the demand for foreign produce, and people who may not have grown up eating tropical foods, like me, have also developed a taste for them. One of my favourite ways to warm up in the winter is with a bowl of sambar, a spicy lentil soup with those same imported drumsticks you eat by sucking the pulp and seeds from their long, hard shells. My wintertime warming elixir, originally from subtropical Sri Lanka, one of the hottest places on earth, may not have been intended to heat chilled bones in a frigid climate, but it adapts well to Canada.

Thankfully, exciting innovation is taking place at universities and research centres across the country as people investigate new ways to grow a wider variety of fruits and vegetables in greenhouses, hoping to expand our local industry beyond the traditional tomato, cucumber and sweet pepper. There is potentially big money to be made by satisfying a local market for tropical vegetables that farmers wouldn't ever be able to grow here without the help of glass or plastic. At the Pacific Agri-Food

Research Centre, David Ehret has figured out how to grow berries in the winter. He starts the raspberry plants outside in pots in the summer, and then, in November, after the canes become dormant, he brings them inside, cutting short this period of the plant's cycle. He then introduces the plants to light and heat earlier in the season than they would be in nature, thus forcing them to blossom and then fruit in February and March. While no one in Canada is growing winter raspberries on a commercial level yet, at least one greenhouse in Florida is producing organic strawberries.

In Canada people are already growing tropical produce under glass. One such enterprise is the Glasbergen Greenhouses, a family-run operation in Fenwick, Ontario, that has gone from growing flowers to producing bitter melon primarily for the Asian market in Toronto. Bitter melon looks like a big, long, spiky cucumber, a little like an alligator. In English it is named bitter for good reason. People across Asia, South Asia and the West Indies eat the melon in part for its medicinal properties; some say it is a blood cleanser and good for diabetics. In Toronto there is a huge demand for the stuff, a demand that has traditionally been filled by imports from the Dominican Republic and Honduras that are flown or shipped here. Glasbergen is the only greenhouse in the country growing bitter melon. They are able to produce them year-round by heating their greenhouses with a biomass boiler system that burns organic matter such as wood waste, mouldy beans, corn and grains.

Before going commercial with the crop, Glasbergen experimented with the plant for almost four years, potting seedlings in the back corner of the greenhouse in secret to perfect their method. So far the business is going really well because, although their bitter melons cost a little more than the imported ones, the quality of the locally grown ones is far superior, and not just because the melons have been grown in a controlled environment. Bitter melon starts to deteriorate the moment it is harvested, and imports can take up to a week before landing in a Canadian supermarket. Glasbergen, on the other hand, can ship them to the stores the day after they are picked. Production and sales have gone so well that the company is now interested in seeing what other tropical vegetables might thrive in a greenhouse here.

Another innovation that scientists in Canada hope to develop into a sustainable food-production system for greenhouses is called aquaponics, which combines aquaculture with hydroponics to create a closed-loop system that produces both fish and vegetables. "How to produce food the most efficient way?" asked Nick Savidov, a researcher at the Agriculture and Rural Development research station in Brooks, Alberta. "Spending as little resources as possible to save fresh water and save our environment. That's aquaponics." You start with big tanks in which fish are farmed for food. The water in which they swim is circulated through a system that uses bacteria to clean the water and dissolve the nutrients in the fish waste to fertilize the plants. "We are building a system where nothing goes out but food," he said. In the seven years during which his team produced tons of tilapia and vegetables like bok choy, cucumber and coriander, they didn't change the water once. They added fertilizers, and the system produced absolutely no waste. They did use power to run the pumps, but are looking into using solar panels to generate energy. Also, they are working on a project with low-energy LED lights to reduce their energy consumption. Israel, a country where water is scarce, is supporting research into aquaponics. In the United States, a few commercial aquaponics operations are already up and running, and Savidov predicts people will soon start them here too. "I regard aquaponics as the technology of the future," he said. "This is coming to agriculture."

.

All this technology and ingenuity brings hope and exciting prospects for an array of local foods in Canada year-round, but the truth is that no greenhouse is sustainable unless it is economically viable. And what rules the economics of the greenhouse is not only the input costs (heat, light and fertilizer) but the price of the competitor's produce at the grocery store. While Canada currently has the largest greenhouse industry, Mexico's, albeit a fledgling industry, is growing. Although most greenhouses there tend to be low-technology operations, using often not more than plastic sheeting and two-by-fours to cover hectares and hectares of land to grow tomatoes, some newer operations are similar to Canadian ones and have the potential to produce a steady stream of produce. Considering the amount of investment in this industry in Mexico, many believe this is a growth area. And the cheaper the prices of imports, the less chance our own greenhouses have to take off.

A few weeks after my visit to Jo Slegers's farm, I was in my local natural foods store. It was almost Christmas, and only a few Ontario root vegetables—carrots, Jerusalem artichokes, parsnips—were on display beside the green lineup of imports like bunched kale, spinach, even dandelion greens. There was a heap of organic greenhouse peppers from Israel that likely took a jumbo jet to get here, and some greenhouse tomatoes trucked up from Mexico. Such is the state of the local food economy in an Ontario December, when our main greenhouses have shut down for a few winter months until the sun shines a little stronger in these parts.

Then, over in the corner, a familiar red-and-white logo caught my eye. Almost hidden in a basket were Slegers's greens. A half-dozen heads of Boston lettuce, slightly droopy, were waiting for someone to pick them up, which I did, knowing that Jo is one of the few people growing around here at this time of year. One Boston lettuce with its buttery leaves, this softness characteristic of its greenhouse origins, cost me $2.95. The organic red oak-leaf lettuce from California was priced at $2.59.

The walk home was cold and I struggled to wade through the knee-high banks of snow while carrying my groceries. It's usually summer when I walk home with locally grown vegetables. There was something exciting about packing Jo's greens on that icy day. The experience allowed me to imagine a time when this kind of purchase is matter-of-fact, something everyone does because we have greenhouse production that supplies us with food during the winter.

At home, I assembled a local salad for lunch. The lettuce I topped with some sheep's feta made on the outskirts of the city, along with red pepper I'd roasted and frozen at the end of the summer. I thought of the steps that Slegers's greens had taken from farmer to consumer that I had been fortunate to witness. I knew that this lettuce started with a seed in a plug inside a black tray before it was moved to the hydroponic troughs in the greenhouse and then on to a truck en route to the store near my house, where I placed it in my shopping bag and then took it home to my kitchen. I knew every single link in this food chain—how unlike so many of the other faceless products we pick up in the anonymous aisles and bring home. And it was winter. A season during which I figured, not so long ago, we had no choice but to depend on imports or else revert to the pioneer diet of potatoes, onions and more potatoes. There is hope for a future food system in Canada that can feed us nutritious, green foods through the winter months, without interruption. On that day, the hope for the future took shape in a Boston lettuce salad with feta and roasted red pepper doused in a maple-syrup vinaigrette.

I then spent lunch dreaming of tending to a greenhouse in my own backyard and imagined greenhouses all over the city, structures that can merge the farm and the metropolis.

PART TWO

. . .

IN
THE
CITY

CHAPTER FIVE

COWS IN THE CITY, CROPS DOWNTOWN
Turning the City into a Farm in British Columbia

I f Harold and Kathy Steves didn't round up their cows and herd them into the barnyard when the tide comes in, the animals would be swept out to sea. The couple has posted a tide chart in their kitchen window to help them keep track of the water levels at the mouth of the Fraser River, in front of their thirty-three-acre farm. When the water swells, it can submerge most of the Steveses' land—only the house, the barn and a bit of pasture keep dry, protected by a wide dyke. The water inches up slowly, gradually swallowing the grassy pasture where the cows graze. On the farm, there are constant reminders that you are at the edge of the Pacific Ocean: widgeon ducks and snow geese pick through the bulrushes and sea grasses, the smell of salt is intermingled with the whiff of cow manure, and from inside the house built in 1917 by Harold Steves's grandfather, you can see the grey waters stretching out past these tidal flats.

And yet the farm's proximity to the rising tides isn't the only unusual aspect of the Steveses' farm. Not only are they perched at the edge of the water with merely a dyke keeping their cows safe, if you stand at the foot of their driveway with your back to the water, you see a typical suburban streetscape. Stretching east from their property is not more farmland but a subdivision. Driveways and manicured bushes and large houses line a wide boulevard that has retained its rural roots only in name: Steveston Highway. The road looks like any other prosperous suburb in North America, with cars zipping off to the mall and people biking to work and out for a stroll with their dogs. The Steveses' farm is located in the city of Richmond, part of the Greater Vancouver Regional District. It's a relic of a time when the land around these parts was used for food production and pasture for dairy cows.

While theirs may be the only farm left in the area, the rest having disappeared thirty-odd years ago, the farm isn't a keepsake from a bygone era. It's not a memento that evokes nostalgia for a time when agriculture was quaint and pastoral. Rather, the Steveses' farm is a symbol for the future and a functioning example of how cities and farms, of all shapes and sizes, can coexist. The Steveses' farm shows us how we can start to balance urban food production in the city with the periurban agriculture that takes place on the outskirts of urban centres as we move towards a sustainable food system. The next step in building a local food system is the city itself. Urban agriculture can help to make local eating a reality in Canada.

Harold Steves came out to meet me in his house slippers when I arrived at the family farm one early morning in January. He had finished cleaning the stalls in the barn and was just making coffee. Kathy bent over a bucket of feed in the barnyard, mixing the last of the morning's barley for the cows. It was a cool, grey day. The dew was heavy on the grass and the air was damp. Fog had wrapped itself around the farm, making the house and the small wooden barn not far behind it look as if they were on an island. The thick fog had been hanging around for almost a week, but Harold didn't mind. "Actually, it's great with the fog. You can't see the neighbours," he said, chuckling to himself. The hazy screen took the farm back in time to when Harold lived there as a boy, before the fields were taken over by subdivisions, before the city surrounded the place.

Every morning at about eight, Harold and Kathy head outside to take care of their herd of Belted Galloways, a rare breed of cow that is black with a white stripe separating the forelegs from the hind; some people call them Oreo cookies. With their long, curly hair and big, round ears that stick out, the cows reminded me of teddy bears. There are thirty of them on the farm, if you include the calves. Every morning, Kathy feeds them a mixture of barley mash and added minerals while Harold does his chores, such as cleaning out the manure, heaping it on a pile in the back to be used later as fertilizer. Then, if the season is right and the tide is out, they lead the cows to pasture.

Where most people would have patio furniture and a barbecue, only a few metres away from their back door is the barn, a stout building with several stalls and a fenced-in yard. Just beyond that is the dyke. To get out of the barnyard and into the grassy fields where the cattle spend their summer daytime hours munching at the sea grasses, they must cross this dyke. They lumber up a wooden bridge and onto the dyke itself, which is nothing more than a mound of earth separating the tidal plains from the land where the new houses have been built. The cows then pass through a gate on the other side and head into the fields.

At the top of the dyke's hump runs a public walking path where hundreds of people—thousands in the summer—pass every day. To alert the public to the cow crossing, the city has erected a yellow caution sign displaying the black silhouette of a cow. (Some creative person has painted a white line around the stomach of the sign's cow in tribute to the Belted Galloways.) A hand-painted placard on the shed closest to the dyke's walking path reads "Natural Beef for Sale."

I visited the Steveses' farm because it provides an example of how a farm can exist in a city. And all the time I was at the farm, I was in a state of amazement. I couldn't help but remain in wonder that I was in a city, that these cows, this barn, this living and breathing organism that is a farm existed *in the city*. I've visited many farms, but none have been as extraordinarily situated as the Steveses'. Harold and Kathy have seen this awe before in their visitors and they graciously showed me around, humouring my surprise. Harold said the neighbours don't mind the cows, even the smell of manure that wafts in the direction of their suburban homes. One woman did complain—she called Harold and asked when the farm was shutting down. "I told her, 'Well, we've been here a hundred years so I figure we'll be here a hundred more,' " he recounted, laughing again. The woman launched a mini protest at Richmond city hall, to no avail. The other neighbours started their own campaign against her anti-agrarian complaints. She eventually moved away. The farm didn't fit into her sanitized vision of a city—precisely the type of vision that is being challenged by the growing field of urban agriculture.

The way I see it, farms like Harold and Kathy's are an important part of a sustainable foodshed. So are community gardens, collective and allotment gardens, food-producing green roofs, city greenhouses, backyard grapevines, front-yard vegetable patches and school gardens—any kind of food production that takes place in the city or the suburbs. This is urban agriculture in the twenty-first century. Rapid urbanization has increased demand for land, and what was once farmland is being stripped of its topsoil, levelled and transformed into building lots. As cities grow, there are more people to feed, yet the farms that produce the food are being pushed farther and farther away by development.

Over the last fifty years, according to Statistics Canada, half of the country's urban growth took over good farmland. The Neptis Foundation, an independent think tank in Toronto that researches urban issues, has been tracking the rate of urbanization in Canada. They've looked at satellite imagery of the land around Toronto, Vancouver and Calgary starting in the 1990s, as well as census data, and found that sprawl continues to spread. We all know what urban sprawl looks like, but the technical definition is housing built at a faster rate than population growth, when housing takes over farmland. Around Calgary, sprawl is most intense, with 78 percent of the city's new construction built on rural land; the phenomenon is so severe there that the city is growing at twice the rate of the population. In Toronto, 56 percent of new homes were built on farmland; the rate for Vancouver is 20 percent.

This is also a global phenomenon. In the United States, it is estimated that during the 1990s, nearly a million acres of agricultural land were turned over to other uses every year. And when we pave over one farmer's field, there isn't an unlimited supply of cultivable soil to replace it. According to the 2005 Millennium Ecosystem Assessment report, 24 percent of the earth's surface is already used for farming; in the past sixty years, humans have converted more land into agricultural soil than in the eighteenth and nineteenth centuries combined.[14] There isn't much more cultivable earth left, and yet to this day, farmland is still being paved over around cities. In recent history, we've overcome this problem by shipping food greater distances, which has meant the average person at the supermarket isn't aware of what's been happening to the fields. We've quickly grown used to spinach from California's Central Valley and blueberries from Chile and only occasionally stop to wonder whatever happened to that farmer who used to sell corn from the back of his truck down by the gas station.

One hundred years ago, more than half of the North American population worked on farms. Now, for the first time in human history, more than half of the world's population lives in urban areas. We have become a society of urbanites, relying on fewer and fewer farmers to feed us. By 2050, the United Nations projects, 70 percent of the world's population will live in cities. Ensuring that all these people are fed in a sustainable manner is a challenge humankind has never faced before. Canada is not yet home to a megacity such as Mumbai or Cairo, teeming with tens of millions of residents, but we do face the pressing question of how to feed in a sustainable way the millions who live in urban settings. And so the city is an important part of a sustainable food system. The decisions made there will have profound effects on every single link in the food chain, from the farm to the garbage dump.

Any food system starts on the farm and includes all the stages of food production and consumption, from processing in mills, dairies, abattoirs and canners to distribution, wholesaling and retail, all the way down the line to consumption and waste. According to Rod MacRae, assistant professor in the Faculty of Environmental Studies at York University, a sustainable food system takes its cues from nature—that is, it acts like an ecosystem and tries to keep everything in balance. "The basic concept is to expend energy and resources as close to consumption points as possible—closed-loop consumption," he said. One major problem with our global food system today is that it takes resources from one region and puts them in another where they end up as sewage and landfill. A sustainable system attempts to close the loop so nutrients cycle in a specific region. While you wouldn't be able to fit an entire food chain in an urban centre—it would be hard to find the room to grow enough grain to feed a megacity amid its population, for example—when an urban centre becomes part of the food loop, its environmental burden lessens. Urban agriculture offers the city a way to minimize its ecological footprint and, at least partly, feed itself.

The environmental imperative to incorporate the city into the food system also offers us a wonderful opportunity to reimagine our urban centres. The potential for urban agriculture to beautify the cityscape, reinforce community and add to our quality of life is significant. According to a report on the health benefits of urban agriculture in the United States, not only do city gardeners save money on food, but when they start to grow their own produce, their overall eating habits improve too. The study also found that cultivating food in the city contributes to mental health by relaxing gardeners, increases people's exercise levels, improves the environment and brings the community together.[15] There can be a financial incentive too. Produce grown by people in their backyards and in community gardens can yield more than $500 a year in vegetables. The benefits are wide reaching.

Imagine living in the suburbs and going for a walk along, say, a dyke like the one near Harold and Kathy's place, or maybe a park or a waterfront trail on a Saturday afternoon and picking up some beef from a farmer you know along the way rather than at the supermarket. Picture what it would be like to look out the window of your condominium downtown and see backyards lined with rows of the leeks, potatoes, beans, carrots and peas you stock up on every week at the farmers' market in your neighbourhood park. Picture a city where warehouse rooftops are transformed into green roofs, where food is grown for hospitals, restaurants, daycare centres. Imagine a city that helps to feed itself, a city that works to minimize the ecological footprint of its food by finding space within its borders for agriculture.

.   .   .

Urban agriculture as a field of study is new to the world. Only a few years ago, *urban* and *agriculture* were antithetical words to most of us. But although we might not have had a popular name for it, urban agriculture has always been part of every Canadian city. I grew up eating cherry tomatoes my grandmother grew outside her kitchen door and collecting mulberries from the tree in our backyard. All over downtown Toronto, you will find trellises thick with grape vines planted decades ago by European immigrants who wanted to continue to make their own wine in the new country, as well as grow tomatoes, cucumbers and peppers in their backyards. Next door to where I live, there are trellises of a different kind, shoulder height, made out of sticks that Mr. and Mrs. Ma, who are originally from China, use to grow a hanging squash. A few blocks away on the main street near Chinatown, other families coax giant zucchini and pumpkins and eggplants out of the limited soil in their front gardens, sometimes even out of cracks in the concrete. The vines can grow so big in the August sun that they often drape over the curb and onto the side-walk. I wonder if the people in the streetcars riding by notice the mini farms they pass every day.

While many of us here are only now catching on to the environmental benefits of incorporating what we see as rural work into the urban con-text, the rest of the world, particularly the less prosperous parts, already rely on food grown in the city for survival. Poverty, not a vision of sus-tainability, drives residents of places like Accra, Chiang Mai, and Rio de Janeiro to grow food and raise livestock within city limits. In fact, the United Nations Food and Agriculture Organization believes the poten-tial of urban agriculture to be so significant that it created a program in Africa and South America encouraging food production in and around cities. The FAO found that people can grow an enormous amount of food in the city. In the Democratic Republic of Congo, they are converting two thousand acres into allotment gardens in cities such as Kinshasa and Kisangani, to produce fresh vegetables for about eighty thousand people; in the barrios of Bogotá, residents now grow about twenty-five kilograms of produce such as beans and tomatoes every month in all sorts of impro-vised contraptions, including old tires and water bottles.

After Cuba was shut out of the global petroleum economy when the Soviet Union collapsed and the country lost its principal source of for-eign currency, Cubans were forced to wean their society off its depen-dency on fossil fuels. This has had a profound effect on food production. Out of necessity, since they no longer had the gasoline to transport food from the countryside, Cubans developed ways to grow produce in cities and inadvertently became world leaders in urban agriculture. They have become particularly adept at growing organic vegetables in a system they call *organopónicos*, raised beds filled with a mixture of soil and organic materials that are usually farmed cooperatively. These *organopónicos* cover nearly 175,000 acres in cities across the country and grow an impressive 25.8 kilograms of produce per square metre a year without the use of any chemical fertilizers or pesticides. (To put this number in context, in 1994 when Cuba's experiment in urban agriculture was just beginning, they were growing only about 1.5 kilograms a square metre.) Growing food intensively in the city has meant that Cubans use only 5 percent of the energy Canadians do to produce their food.

Cuba might be an extreme example, but some argue that it is simply accomplishing now what the rest of the world may be forced to try when we decide we'd rather use diminishing fossil fuel supplies for purposes other than shipping food we could grow here across oceans and continents. And people outside Cuba are pondering this possibility. A professor in New York City has dreamt up a now famous high-tech solution to urban food production. Dickson Despommier's vertical farms have attracted a lot of attention, more for their novelty than for the potential of these envisioned sky-scraper farms that would operate as controlled environments in which such crops as corn, wheat and bananas could grow year-round in places such as New York.

On the whole, however, the models people in Canada are gravitating towards are decidedly low-tech. In Calgary, the Food Policy Council wants to create thousands of new food-producing gardens to increase the amount of food grown within the city limits. The number of community gardens in Edmonton is increasing as more people take interest in gardening there. Vancouver's city council announced it would aim to start 2,010 community garden plots, the number chosen to reflect the year the city hosts the Olympics. Vancouver has also responded to pressure from residents who want to keep chickens in their backyards by amending bylaws to allow for the practice. It is becoming increasingly popular in cities and towns across the country for people to raise chickens in their yards, whether or not it is allowed. While the practice is permitted in a few places, including Niagara Falls, Brampton and Victoria, most municipalities forbid backyard flocks. But this isn't stopping hundreds of households from secretly supplementing their grocery supplies with eggs they've collected in their own yards. Bonnie Klohn, a chicken advocate in Kamloops, where the backyard chicken movement is particularly active, estimates that about two hundred families in her city alone are breaking the law and risking fines to keep the birds.

All over British Columbia, in such places as Nelson, Victoria and Nanaimo, as well as in Hamilton and Toronto in Ontario, tree fruit projects glean fruit from backyard trees and from parks so it doesn't rot and go to waste. The fruit is often distributed to community organizations such as women's and homeless shelters, and sometimes even turned into products such as apple cider and plum chutney to raise money for a charity. There's also an online backyard-sharing database (sharingbackyards.com), which was started in Victoria, that helps match keen city gardeners with people who want their yards cultivated for food production. Property owners with land to spare post a short description of their garden along with what they want someone to do with their plot so that those yearning to grow something can get in touch.

Montreal is another hot spot for urban agriculture. An extensive network of community gardens, with a long waiting list, thrives, as do *jardins collectifs*, where people plant crops together and share the harvest. A group at the non-profit organization Alternatives has started the Rooftop Garden Project, whose goal is to grow food on roofs, balconies and fire escapes in the city. They've created a container gardening system with a built-in water reservoir to ensure a steady supply of water. Their prototype is a plastic container that resembles a residential recycling box but is filled with earth. Corrugated plastic punctured with holes separates the soil from the water chamber at the bottom.

I visited one of the Rooftop Garden Project's demonstration gardens at the McGill University campus. Dozens of plastic containers of all sorts—used food containers from restaurants, repurposed giant buckets of pickles and old rain barrels, blue boxes, and just about any kind of plastic receptacle—were planted with beans and peas, herbs and eggplants, tomatoes, camomile, kale and lettuce. The plants spilled out of their buckets. Bees pollinated the pea blossoms. The tomato vines that grew up the side of a wall were so long they looked as if they might overtake the building.

The food grown in the rooftop garden is handed out at the food bank run by one of the participating organizations. "There's not much to do aside from pick the food," said Ismael Hautecoeur, the project coordinator, during my visit. It's simply not a lot of work to grow in containers like this—no weeding is necessary, and with the reservoir, not too much watering is required.

I can attest to the simplicity of planting in their boxes. I grew eggplants, tomatoes, lettuce, herbs and one tiny green pepper in two of their growing containers, and it required hardly any effort. I never weeded, and when we went away on vacation, I only had to ask someone to come by and water them once.

The Rooftop Garden Project's creative work has inspired people in Toronto, and the project's growing boxes are being used throughout the city. Also, people from Montreal have travelled to Senegal, Morocco, Mexico and elsewhere to start similar rooftop projects there.

There are also the entrepreneurs for whom urban agriculture has captured the imagination. Like Jean Snow, one of the country's urban-agriculture pioneers, who lives in Dartmouth, a suburb of Halifax. Jean is in her early fifties, with light brown hair, and the day we met she looked like your average suburban mom wearing a blue windbreaker and sunglasses to protect her eyes from the setting autumn sun. In the summer of 2008, Jean had a life-changing moment while reading Barbara Kingsolver's *Animal, Vegetable, Miracle*. She had spent the last eighteen years at home with her kids, whom she has home-schooled, making a little money on the side by, among other things, selling melaleuca—also known as tea tree oil—through a buying club. She read the Kingsolver book in one day, and by nightfall she wanted to plant food in her backyard.

She searched the Internet and learned about urban farming, and within weeks, she and her husband had decided to turn their backyard into a food-producing operation.

Snow is what's called a SPIN farmer, SPIN being an acronym for small plot intensive farming, a system tailored for cities and towns. It transforms backyards, empty lots and otherwise non-producing plots into commercially productive agricultural land that turns a profit. Wally Satzewich and Gail Vandersteen, a Saskatoon couple who now farm about two dozen backyard plots in their city, invented this way of looking at urban farming as a business over a decade ago. They sell their how-to manual online (Snow bought one and has modelled her operation after what they preach). The guide promotes organic, low-input growing methods and helps new farmers set achievable revenue goals, showing them how to grow high-earning crops such as baby salad greens. The SPIN mantra is "Grow what you sell, not sell what you grow," explained Snow. The business model purports to yield about $300 in gross sales per bed each season, amounting to a gross sales income of $120,000 an acre.

Snow is not the only person in Canada to have been inspired by the SPIN model. Across the country, people are turning urban spaces into revenue-generating agricultural plots—backyards, mostly. In Vancouver, you can join an urban-agriculture CSA; while in Victoria, a couple has made a living for several years growing vegetables in a patchwork of city backyards. Nationwide, many more people have turned lawns into food-producing garden beds. Like Snow, these people were attracted to the simplicity of the operation: the land is often free, the inputs are low, it is organic and the market is nearby, often literally next door.

There is nothing fancy about Snow's backyard. It's a good-sized yard with a horse chestnut tree at the back, an old canoe, an upturned wheelbarrow and a rusty old bicycle to the side. The grass has been replaced by five planting rows, each two feet wide and about twenty-five feet long. Jean followed the SPIN guidelines even though the rows are a little too wide for her to straddle comfortably while she picks, since she's only five feet tall. At the side of the house she and her husband have built a washing station where she can rinse greens on large screens and then transfer them to an outdoor fridge to keep the harvest fresh until market day.

"In one planting I just got so much out of it, it's amazing," Jean said on our tour around the garden. "This is romaine, I just harvested it. That's a really neat mesclun. If you look at it, it's so interesting, the colours, the spiky broad leaf." She also grows mâche, radishes, red leaf lettuce, arugula, beets along the fence, and cilantro, basil, oregano, sage and lemon balm, mostly in pots. She harvests on Fridays with scissors, then washes her produce and packages it in small bags to sell the next day at the farmers' market. At her table she posts a sign featuring a logo her daughter designed of a wheelbarrow overflowing with produce; it reads "Chemical-free." She charges $3 for one bag or $5 for two. Once she sold fifty of these small bags in one morning. She also sells her greens to a few restaurants and to a vegetable stand whose owner likes to stock local produce when he can.

"People say, what do you do, and I say, 'I'm an urban farmer.'" She paused and then she smiled. "I'm an urban farmer! It's just so great."

·

People like Snow, ventures like the Rooftop Garden Project and the cross-country backyard chicken movement, and all the other facets of city food production together demonstrate that, while the Canadian urban-agriculture movement might be far behind Cuba's in terms of the quantity of food it produces, we nevertheless are slowly transforming our cities into farms of sorts. We are expanding the definition of agriculture to include urban and periurban food production. And by redefining what belongs in an urban area and what belongs in the country, we are not only creating a new vision of the city but helping to build a fully functional local food system.

Joe Nasr, an associate at the Centre for Studies in Food Security at Ryerson University and one of the founders of the North America–wide MetroAg Alliance for Urban Agriculture, says that urban food systems that rely on both what is produced in the city and food that comes from the farms on the periphery have existed for a long time. Urban populations throughout history, from medieval Europe to China to pre-conquest Mexico, have relied on food grown outside the city walls—this is the origin of periurban agriculture, food grown on the outskirts of a city. "At the same time, it was not unusual back then to have small pockets of agriculture in cities. You had a tradition of raising chickens, livestock right inside the denser cities. So historically, it's nothing new." In Canada too, vegetable- and fruit-producing farms were often clustered on the edges of cities. Around Toronto in the 1880s, there were a number of farms growing vegetables as well as dairy farms that produced the fresh milk people in the city drank every day. Inside the city, residents tended to vegetable gardens and even kept chickens.

Nasr lives in downtown Toronto, and although he doesn't have a vegetable garden of his own, he did plant a fruit tree one spring. The relationship between the city and the land on the urban fringe has changed over time, he said. "The land behind the city, the hinterland, it never completely disappeared. But it got much weaker." Now people are starting to realize the importance of this periurban farmland to a sustainable food system, like Harold Steves's farm in Richmond; you'd be hard pressed to feed a city without it. But rather than recreating the historical notion of hinterland and relying heavily on the farms at the edge of the city for local food production, Nasr suggests that each area play a specific role in the food system. He predicts that in downtown areas, higher-value crops, such as green leaf vegetables and berries, for which people pay a premium, will likely be grown. Their higher price will justify the use of more expensive real estate for food production. (Initiatives like SPIN farming encourage this.) On the edge of the city, where the sprawl gives way to fields, Nasr believes there will be small and mid-sized farms producing vegetables and raising small livestock. "It probably will be very diversified. That's where the bulk of production for the city will be," he said.

On these farms, Nasr anticipates a cultural shift as new farmers start to work the land. "Many periurban farmers who are getting old and retiring, their replacements are going to come from the urban centres," he said. "They are going to bring relationships that are already established. And so naturally, with time, there will be more integration between the urban and the periurban. That will help create relationships that haven't been there over time." These relationships will be the foundation of a new food system. The smaller-scale farming within the city will be supported by what's happening on the urban edge.

At first, it might sound a little far-fetched to think that relationships between farmers and consumers can build a new foodshed, but if you stop to think about it, relationships are exactly what's missing from today's industrial food system. I have no idea who grew the food at my supermarket—not even the oranges that are sold under the Fair Trade banner featuring a generic photo of some peasant somewhere in an attempt to evoke a story and create the illusion of exactly this relationship (marketers know the value of this connection). Even the origins of the chicken I roasted recently for dinner are a complete mystery to me, despite its being labelled a "naturally raised" bird. I don't know who tended it, let alone where it lived, what it ate or how it was butchered—or even when it was butchered.

Conversely, I have a relationship with the potatoes I popped into the pan to sizzle in the fat. They were grown by my dad, so I obviously know where they came from, how they were grown and that they were free from chemicals. I even know that the manure used for the compost comes from grass-fed cows that are free of antibiotics. And when I run out of my dad's spuds, I buy more from a farmer named Ted Thorpe, whose thirty-two-acre periurban farm is less than an hour's drive away. He's a friendly guy, with curly red hair and freckles, who is usually barefoot at the farmers' market where I've bought his produce for years. He was one of the first organic farmers in the area a couple of decades ago, and I'm confident that the dusty potatoes he sells are chemical-free. Not only are they certified organic, but Thorpe has told me about his farm and how he works there and I trust this living and breathing person with whom I chat every week. This connection to the source of my potatoes is satisfying. I take more pleasure in eating them. I feel better knowing the farmer who grew them; I feel like I am part of something bigger. The potato isn't just a potato; it is a piece of culture and tradition.

Let's take this one step further. If I don't know who grew the potato or how it was grown, then the potato becomes just a thing, a commodity, an object to roast and to eat. But if I have a connection to how my potato is grown, then I am more likely to be aware that this potato started in the soil, that earthworms slinked by its underground home, fertilizing the earth, that the plant's leaves collected nutrients from the sun's energy and sent this food down to the potato that the farmer dug and then sold to me. When I am aware of this series of events that produced my food, then I am suddenly aware of my place in the natural cycle. I am part of a larger ecosystem instead of simply being a consumer.

But this is all pretty philosophical and intangible, surely not a concrete pillar in a food system. Or is it?

Sustainable agriculture specialist Kent Mullinix would say that these, in fact, are important emotions and an integral part of a food system. "Agriculture is about community and community is about agriculture," he said. "Working on urban agriculture is synonymous with working on a sustainable agri-food system. It's all connected. I can't help but think that developing a healthy agri-food system is to develop an urban-focused element, thereby connecting 95 percent of the North American population to their food system." Mullinix is a pomologist by training who, after working with apples, ended up in sustainable agriculture in Washington State for several decades before immigrating with his family to Canada in 2007. He now works at Vancouver's Kwantlen Polytechnic University. Although he spent a large part of his career working with rural farms, now that he is living in a city for the first time in his life, he sees in multi-dimension the importance of locating agriculture in the city precisely because of the opportunity for nurturing the relationship between the grower and the eater, between food and the consumer, between nature—the original source of everything we eat—and society.

"We've become so detached from what it really is to be human," he says. "Why is eating not connected with providing sustenance to our spiritual self? And helping us to define what it is to be human? Every person is connected with food and with the agri-food system and they are in fact part of it. That is the promise of urban agriculture. It's connecting every-one with food in meaningful ways that transforms their perceptions of the natural world. To me, this is what being an agriculturalist is all about. It's about relationships."

To coax these relationships along, Mullinix is involved in a num-ber of initiatives in the Vancouver area. For one, he is helping to start a farm school to train a new generation of people to produce, distrib-ute and market food grown in the city. The Municipality of Richmond has donated a plot of land to be used, likely for incubator farms, just a few kilometres away from Harold Steves's farm. On the edge of the city where the subdivisions peter out, Mullinix is also helping to plan a com-munity that a developer wants to build on the edge of the Fraser River. Mullinix says that if it goes ahead, it would be the model for what he calls agricultural urbanism.

The Southlands project, proposed for one of the last swaths of unde-veloped land, is in the Tsawwassen area south of Vancouver, which is dot-ted with subdivisions, strip malls and Tim Hortons franchises. Right now, it's a controversial project because the land is currently protected by the province's Agricultural Land Reserve, which prohibits development in perpetuity. If the project were to go ahead, however, in the way Mullinix envisions, it would be home to about five thousand people. One-third of the 600 acres would be green space, one-third would be used for housing, and the last 225 acres would be allotted to organic food production, said Mullinix. People who buy homes in the development would be choosing to live in a community that incorporates agriculture into every aspect of life. Instead of two-car garages, each housing plot would have space for vegetable gardens. The farmers who work the 225 acres of land would be their neighbours, he said, and the agricultural land would be legally protected from future development.

Building agriculture into a development links the viability of the community directly to the farms; urban living can intimately support agriculture. The Southlands project is still a long way from getting the go-ahead. It may never be realized on that piece of land. But at the very least, the plans for this development might help us to redefine the suburbs, transforming urban sprawl into urban agriculture.

But not everybody wants to transform the city into a farm. While many people are working hard to increase food production in urban centres, some of their neighbours aren't pleased with their plans. It comes down to a philosophical difference—that the city should exist separately from nature and from the farm. Many believe that the city should *not* produce food; not everyone wants chickens in the neighbours' backyards. When an orchard was planned for a park in midtown Toronto, some residents objected because they feared the mess the fallen fruit would create. In Halifax, the city ordered Louise Hanavan to dispose of the three laying hens she was keeping in her backyard after a neighbour complained about an alleged rat problem. In Surrey, British Columbia, where homeowners are allowed to keep a small number of chickens if their property spans at least one acre, officials forced one family to give away their birds because their lot didn't meet the criteria. And in London, Ontario, the owner of a twenty-three-acre farm where he keeps horses and cows is fighting to save his property after city council voted to rezone the land as non-agricultural because developers have built apartment buildings in the fields that not long ago surrounded the farm.

Conflicts like these are not new. This case of the London farmer who watched the city creep up to his fencelines and then found himself being told that it is *he* who does not belong echoes the battle that Harold Steves fought to keep his property in the face of advancing urbanization.

.

Harold Steves's family has been farming the piece of land abutting the Fraser River Delta since 1877, when Manoah and Martha Steves, his great-grandfather and great-grandmother, arrived here from out east. The land they settled was nothing more than swamp with plenty of mosquitoes and bulrushes. The family had to build their house on stilts to keep it safe from the tides until they had completed a dyke to hold the waters back. By 1937, when Harold was born, they ran a mixed farm with some crops to feed the cows and horses, pigs and a staggering two thousand chickens. It was Harold's job as a boy to brave their beaks and stick his hands into the nests looking for eggs. The family also ran a dairy operation, producing milk and butter for the community. Manoah had imported Holsteins and opened the first dairy farm on the Lower Mainland.

During Harold's childhood, the community around him was made up of farmers and fishermen; some locals were employed in the cannery in nearby Steveston (named after Manoah himself) and the rest worked in the fields. The townspeople built a wharf where a paddle-wheeler could load up with the farmers' vegetables and ship them to market in Victoria. It was old-fashioned family-farm living, and Harold grew up with absolutely no inkling of how the landscape would change over his lifetime. "It was totally rural. In the thirties, forties and fifties, my guess is that it wasn't much different from when the pioneers came," he said.

After the Second World War, life around Steveston started to change. Veterans returned from Europe with dreams of farming, and a large area in central Richmond was divided into 1.6-acre plots for the men and their families. Then, around 1958, one of the farmers in the area with the most land (he had amassed his acreage by buying out bankrupted farmers for $10 an acre in the Depression, said Harold) sold to a developer. "My parents were really upset one day reading the newspaper that Les Gilmore was selling his farm for housing," remembered Harold. "Suddenly he was selling hundreds and hundreds of acres. No one could understand why. Why would you put housing on that good land?"

Things changed quickly after that. The city built roads and subdivisions and then assessed the remaining farms as residential rather than agricultural, which meant that farmers couldn't afford the taxes on the land—residential assessments were far higher than what they had been paying. It was a tactic the municipality used to make way for new development and push the farmers out. "Ten years and it was gone. Everybody sold. They had no choice," said Harold. The Steveses' was the sole farm to survive, and only because of a geographic oddity. Eighty of the farm's acres were located on the other side of the dyke in the tidal marsh, and it was not possible to build a subdivision there. At twenty-one, Harold, who'd gone to the University of British Columbia to study agriculture, called the city and argued that the land must maintain its farming status. They acquiesced. Despite this success, it was only the first battle in a fifteen-year-long fight to ensure that he could continue to farm, despite the spectre of the encroaching city.

The experience pushed Harold into his side career as a politician. In 1968, Harold was elected to Richmond City Council, and his professional fight to save farmland began. Over the next four years, he and a colleague in the NDP drafted what was to become British Columbia's Agricultural Land Commission Act, which created the province's Agricultural Land Reserve. The ALR ensures that farmland would be preserved by designating areas of land as agricultural, where farming would be encouraged and non-agricultural uses controlled. This was the first attempt in North America to protect farmland from urban development. The effort has preserved the remaining farmland in the heavily populated areas of British Columbia where demand for real estate has skyrocketed. In fact, according to the Northwest Environment Watch in the United States, the ALR is credited with having kept Vancouver free of the type of sprawl that stretches around other West Coast cities, such as Seattle. Today, the ALR encompasses just under 12 million acres, including forests, small farms and large acreages that are both publicly and privately owned.

The reserve has made possible a food system that has both urban and periurban components in the Greater Vancouver Area. People who live in Vancouver have access to a substantial amount of food grown around their city, and many businesses, such as restaurants, depend on local farmers. The ALR has also provided an example for other regions, such as Ontario's Golden Horseshoe, where a 1.8-million-acre greenbelt was created in 2005. There is one other Canadian greenbelt, around Ottawa, which the National Capital Commission started to assemble in the 1950s, but it is not considered a success because it didn't restrict suburban development and instead pushed sprawl farther away from the city rather than intensifying construction within its borders.

According to Burkhard Mausberg, president of Friends of the Greenbelt Foundation, a non-profit organization dedicated to promoting and preserving Ontario's greenbelt, when a government takes steps to protect land with legislation, they are helping to secure a local food supply. "It maintains the farms," he said. "A farm can't be converted into concrete. As a result, you have a much larger chance of having the opportunity to feed the local residents." Such protection also offers other environmental benefits to society, what is called ecological goods and services. The forests and the grasses and the crops in the fields sequester carbon, the wetlands act as natural water treatment facilities, and air pollution is improved when trees filter out fine particulate and chemicals that contribute to smog. Greenbelts aren't only found in Canada; they exist in the Netherlands, the United Kingdom and Germany as well as in the United States.

Some people—developers in particular—don't like saving farmland. In British Columbia, opponents to the ALR call it the Green Wall. "That's a mild statement," said Harold. "Generally it has expletives attached." Thousands of acres of ALR have been removed from the land bank over the years and turned into housing, commercial and industrial developments; 1,600 acres have been lost in the city of Richmond alone. Developers with a plan and title to the land need only to find sympathetic politicians on local council when they apply to exempt their project from the reserve, and the land is withdrawn from farming forever.

Even with the ALR in effect, the fight to preserve farmland in British Columbia has been Harold's life project. He sat as an NDP member of the province's Legislative Assembly for three and a half years, and then on Richmond city council for three decades. At the age of seventy-one, at the end of 2008, he was re-elected to Richmond council, winning the seat as a candidate who would ensure that the last piece of ALR-protected land in the centre of Richmond would remain that way. Harold feels like it's been a bit of a marathon. Yet he does believe that change is coming. He and Kathy have a waiting list for their beef, and he gets the sense that, finally, people are beginning to realize that farmland is a finite resource that needs to be protected. "I've always been known as an environmentalist. Suddenly the rest of the world has caught up and they say, 'He's right!'"

During my visit to the farm, Harold, Kathy and I took a walk around the perimeter of the garden. They pointed out the few small beds where they grow much of the vegetables they eat. They cultivate a variety of heirloom vegetables, such as something called a mangel, a giant beet that grows to about five kilograms, as well as a rare variety of cauliflower, the Walcheren, and twenty-six types of apples. They've started their own urban-agriculture experiment and are trying to figure out which five varieties of apples a family could grow in their backyard to ensure a supply of homegrown fruit all year round. They pointed out the yellow transparents that are the first to come out, the snow apples that ripen later and keep well into spring, the Wealthy, which are good for baking, as well as the Kathy, a variety they've created themselves.

Then we stopped in the middle of the yard, and Harold leaned back on his heels. He looked the part of the ageing radical with his cowboy boots, his fur-lined jean jacket and his wispy long grey hair. He started to reminisce. Years ago, he said, "there was only one house between here and the airport. Now there's about thirty thousand houses. On a clear day, you could watch the planes landing. To the east, it was all farmland up to No. 1 Road, and the field down the other side was a cabbage patch, which is now a condo development. Steveston actually had cows on the town site." While everybody now knows that Harold and Kathy aren't going anywhere, it used to be that real estate agents would drop in regularly to try to convince them to sell. "A real estate guy came through and said, 'Why don't you sell this place? You could retire on a beach in Florida.' I said, 'I'm retired and I live on a beach. What more could I want?'

"They can't figure out why I'd want to farm in the city. The city has moved in around us. We started as a country farm and now we're an urban farm. We've gone from rural agriculture to urban agriculture, all on the same farm."

.

After I left Harold's farm, I headed over to Richmond City Hall to a meeting of the Richmond Agricultural Advisory Committee, one of the many food-related committees Harold sits on. A woman named Arzeena Hamir, the coordinator of the Richmond Food Security Society and a SPIN farmer, was giving a presentation about pocket markets, tiny farmers' markets set up once a week for a short time in areas where there isn't access to fresh, local food. Hamir was telling the farmers on the committee about the previous summer's success.

The meeting took place in a room on an upper floor with enormous windows overlooking a commercial strip in Richmond. The view is of a large parking lot and the massive expanse of flat roof that covers a mall with a Hudson's Bay store—several football fields' worth of roof. Before the meeting began, the farmers chatted about business and the weather. The conversation lagged, and one of the farmers looked out the window at the mall below. "Harold, look," he said, pointing outside. "There's a hell of a lot of space on the roof over there. You could grow things!" He laughed at what he perceived to be a joke. For him, a traditional farmer, the thought of growing food in the city was absurd.

"Yeah, green roofs," Harold said, nodding. He smiled, but for a different reason. For him it wasn't funny, it was genius. Underneath that mall are the remains of what used to be a farmer's field when Harold was young. If you can't tear down the mall and rip up the asphalt lot to expose this land once again, then why *not* cover the mall with what was there before? Why *not* turn the mall's roof into a green and lush urban garden?

And it was there, as I looked out that window and imagined farmers on the roof of the mall, watering their tomato plants, weeding a bed of beans, that I saw how the various pieces of urban agriculture fit together. The answer to a sustainable food system lies in thousands of smaller answers. The backyard farming businesses like Jean Snow's in Halifax, Harold and Kathy Steves's periurban cattle, and the new farmers whom Kent Mullinix will soon be training. The rooftop gardens in Montreal and the backyard chickens in Surrey. When we live *with* our food, we become part of the cycle.

CHAPTER SIX

LOCAL FOOD FOR THE MILLIONS
Feeding Toronto

The arm of the front security gate at the Ontario Food Terminal is never still for long. All day and night it levers up and down, barely pausing in between each of the hundreds of trucks that arrive one after the other at the gates. Sometimes, at two in the morning, when things start to get really busy, there's an early-morning traffic jam, with eighteen-wheelers, tractor-trailers and cube trucks snaking out far past the gates. In one day, these trucks bring in more than 2.2 million kilograms of fruits and vegetables, a gargantuan amount of food grown by farmers around the world, some as close as a hundred kilometres away, others as far as Malaysia, all to feed the people of Toronto and the surrounding area.

The terminal is the epicentre of the food system for Canada's largest city. It's a creation of the modern food economy, a place where farmers, wholesalers, grocers and restaurateurs come together to form a network of people all preoccupied with feeding fresh fruits and vegetables to the millions living in close quarters, far away from the fields that nourish them.

Toronto's terminal is a hub unlike any other in North America, possibly the world. New York City, Los Angeles and Chicago have larger food terminals, but their management come here to study the way Toronto does it, to learn the secret of how to ensure an utterly smooth operation. There are more than a hundred forklifts and three hundred power machines, small motorized vehicles that haul produce around the place, and eighty thousand square feet of cold storage to preserve the food, the temperature set to hover just above freezing. Positioned around the premise's forty-three acres are dozens of security cameras to monitor the goings-on between the sellers and the thousands of wholesale buyers (chefs, grocers, middlemen called jobbers) who pay for a permit to frequent the terminal. Even with all this activity, the complex produces a mere 10 million kilograms of waste a year, because of a recycling program overseen by a sinuous man named Mr. Park, who ensures that wood crates and waxed boxes are used to heat nearby greenhouses, that rotting vegetable matter is turned into hog feed and that plastics and cardboards are recycled. Needless to say, it's a busy place. For only a few hours at the end of the night, when the wholesalers have gone home and the new shipments haven't yet arrived, the floors are cleaned, the loading docks hosed down and quiet lingers.

It was only about nine in the morning when I visited, but Ron Mandryk had already sold all the Sicilian eggplants and most of the yellow peppers he'd trucked in that day. He had pulled into the Terminal just before two o'clock in the morning, and within seconds, buyers were badgering him, trying to place their orders for his eggplants, shiny, purple globes about the size of bowling balls. A few hours later, after the sun had come up, he still had about a dozen bushels of the peppers, selling for $18 (the Mennonite farmer down the way was selling his for $10), but everything was going fast.

Mandryk, who is a short man of about sixty with greying hair and a bristly, unshaven face, stood at a makeshift desk shaded by an old patio umbrella, cigarette hanging out of his mouth, and tried to manage the chaos. One man with shaggy brown hair, who looked like he should be making a drug deal rather than buying fresh vegetables, stuffed a wad of twenties into Mandryk's hand while another, seated at the desk, badgered him for an answer to a billing question. Yet another poked his head through the empty shelves at the back of the stand and yelled, "Banana?"

"What?" shouted Mandryk over his shoulder.

"Banana!"

"Banana?" Mandryk is particularly well known for his top-quality sweet and hot banana peppers.

"Banana!"

"Not today!"

"Tomorrow?"

"Yeah! How many?"

The man placed his order and Mandryk made a note. He would call his wife, Cindy, who oversees the pickers during the day at the farm; she would make sure they harvested just the right amount to pack on the trucks that evening for the next day's trip to the terminal.

Mandryk is one of more than three hundred farmers who have a stall at the market and who drive their own produce in every day; he has his very own twenty-two-foot truck for the job. It's a two-and-a-quarter hour drive from his farm in Simcoe County, north of Toronto, where he has been growing vegetables for market since he was a teenager. Mandryk's first trip to the terminal was in 1967, when he was only sixteen. His father, a tobacco farmer, had recently passed away, and Ron had been left alone on the farm with his mom. She asked him if he wanted to go into produce or stick with tobacco. He chose produce, and that October he came to the terminal with his first harvest of pumpkins.

These days, he normally arrives six mornings a week with about five hundred bushels of peppers and eggplants—or, earlier in the summer, with cabbages and potatoes—that he grows on his hundred-odd acres of farmland. It's a profitable business, and the family is doing well. They've paid off the farm and the equipment, and have only an $80,000 mortgage left on the barn—an unusually good financial situation for a family farm in Canada. And even though he's coming on retirement age and he and Cindy have talked about slowing things down, the business keeps growing, by 10 to 15 percent every year. They are even able to hire local pickers for slightly higher than the going wage.

But life is not easy. During harvest season, Mandryk sleeps a mere twenty-five hours a week, catching some rest between about five-thirty and ten-thirty each night and spending most of the time the rest of us are tucked into our beds driving his truck to market and then sitting under his dusty patio umbrella, selling his vegetables. Still, he said he wouldn't go anywhere else: the terminal is where he can make the most money. He simply couldn't push the same volume at a farmers' market, and he has built a strong reputation for his produce, for which local grocers will pay a premium. The terminal is, for Mandryk, the ultimate regional marketplace.

The role the food terminal plays in the modern city is an important one, but it is not alone in distributing the food we eat in the city; entire industries exist to accomplish the same task. Supermarkets and restaurant supply companies are also focused on moving food into urban areas, and a vast amount of infrastructure exists to assist them. Add to this even more food that is imported directly by food service companies to feed people in hospitals, universities, corporate cafeterias, prisons and other institutions. That's a whole lot of product coming into our urban centres every day through various channels. And even though the food has likely been on one long journey from farm to, eventually, your fork, it remains remarkably cheap. Food in Canada is, in fact, among the cheapest in the world. According to U.S. Department of Agriculture figures, we in Canada spend an average of 11.68 percent of our income on food, compared with people in France at 15.34 percent, for example, and Vietnam at 64.75 percent.

The challenge for a regional food system is to figure out how to feed the majority of Canadians, who live far away from the fields. To crack this puzzle is to gain an understanding of how a city of the future might be fed.

. . .

The Ontario Food Terminal was opened by the provincial government in 1954 and was modern and efficient, a product of the twentieth century. The post–Second World War boom, with rising population and rising incomes in tandem with the advent of the suburb and the grocery store, had made farmers' markets seem terribly old-fashioned. Up until 1954, the centre of the city's food commerce was near the lakefront, at the downtown St. Lawrence Market. In the early 1950s, farmers still came with their carts, often pulled by horses. There was the squawking of live chickens and turkeys and the stench of unrefrigerated fish peddled by fishmongers, made worse in the summer by the stifling heat; the place was both cacophonous and a stinking mess. Nearby was another whole-sale market, in an old train station, where you could purchase fruit from Niagara that had been shipped to the city by boat.

In the eyes of politicians of the day, such as Frederick Gardiner, then chairman of the municipality of the City of Toronto, the disorganized and unsanitary market was in dire need of modernization. The people of Toronto needed more than a market; they needed a terminus, a symbol of the modern economy. So the provincial government created the Ontario Food Terminal Board, an arm's-length agency that has ever since run the central distribution point.

Today, it is not just local farmers like Ron Mandryk who come to sell their goods. Dozens of wholesalers offer a mix of local and imported produce from the chilled warehouses in the terminal. Many of the trucks passing through the front gates are in fact arriving with their goods from distant locations in the United States—such as California, which is seventy-two hours away by truck, and Florida, a twenty-four-hour journey. Texas is forty-eight hours away, and it takes twelve hours from Philadelphia's port, where the produce has likely been unloaded from a massive freighter that has travelled around the globe. This ensures a constant supply of fresh fruits and vegetables twelve months of the year, as well as exotic fruits such as tamarind and pomelo that don't grow in Canada.

Because the terminal facilitates the trade in long-distance foods, it is often criticized for being an obstacle to local food in Toronto. But not everybody sees it that way. Bruce Nicholas, the terminal's general manager, believes that the terminal already plays an integral role in the local food system in Ontario. Because it provides a market for people such as Mandryk, it supports the region's family farms.

Nicholas—known to many as Mr. Nicholas—met me in the farmers' market section of the terminal, a large area that is shaded by an above-ground parking deck. At about nine in the morning, the rising sun slanting through the lattice of the parking deck started to warm the cold concrete below. The real bustle of the morning had already passed, but it was still busy. Cellphones rang across the market and wheels screeched constantly as the power machines raced about delivering orders to the buyers' trucks. It was harvest season in Ontario, and a cornucopia of local produce was on offer: tomatoes, plums, lettuces, bulbous celery root by the box, bushels of baby pumpkins, mushrooms still earthy and moist, beets as big as softballs and covered with soil, leeks bundled in threes and delicate blackberries resting in tiny boxes. And the smells: first there was the fresh dill plants that were so tall they towered over me and reminded me of my favourite summer potato salad; then it was the basil, displayed like cut flowers in buckets of water, that I could smell from several metres away.

The dozens of farmers who had brought all this to market in the wee hours stood wearily in front of their stands, leaning on boxes of potatoes, resting on the backs of their trucks, waiting to sell their goods to whomever would take them; they'd rather not drive back to the farm with anything in their truck. But as Nicholas "walked the market," pacing up and down the aisles checking out what was for sale, wearing a smile and a lemon-yellow jacket, it was a meet-and-greet. "Good morning, Dave!" and "Hello, John!" he said, waving. "Morning, Grant. Feeling better?" He knew everyone.

Nicholas has worked at the terminal since the 1970s and is mightily proud of what they do here. Running this place, he said, is a public service: they are ensuring the people of Toronto have an uninterrupted supply of affordable fresh food, and they provide the farmers with the opportunity to sell directly to the buyer, without having to go through a middleman. "Here you have a facility where the growers have access to buyers on a wholesale basis," he said, stopping near a potato farmer's neatly stacked boxes. "Our food is diverse and cheap compared to world prices. That pack," he said, pointing to a stack of the boxed potatoes, "that pack can compete with produce from anywhere in the world because he's got an outlet here." Not only does the food terminal give the farmers the chance to sell large quantities of food directly to grocers, it offers a variety of small businesses—from mom-and-pop fruit stands to ethnic food shops to mid-sized greengrocers—the opportunity to become players in the urban food chain, providing competition for the big-box grocery stores in town that have their own networks for procuring food. Nicholas believes the Ontario Food Terminal is an important part of any local food system.

·

But other cities in Canada don't have a food terminal, and so the majority of urban Canadians rely on supermarkets to import food into the city. In places where there isn't a central terminus for food distribution, it's the large supermarkets that bring in the fruits and vegetables via their suppliers around the world. Two major companies have dominated the Canadian grocery industry since the early twentieth century: Loblaw, which runs a number of grocery chains, including Fortinos, the Real Canadian Superstore, Atlantic Superstore and Your Independent Grocer (which isn't what its name implies), and Metro, the Montreal-based retailer that purchased Dominion in 2005 and operates chains such as Food Basics, A&P, Loeb and Marché Richelieu. Even bigger box stores like Walmart and Costco are now competing for the consumer, and every kind of retail enterprise seems to be selling food. Drugstores offer milk, eggs, frozen waffles and packaged soups. You can pick up relish and Kraft Dinner for a buck at the dollar store.

Whereas you buy toothpaste and tchotchkas only so often, you must buy enough food so you can eat at least three times a day. Each customer represents about $6,000 worth of food sales per year, said Nick Jennery, president and CEO of the Canadian Council of Grocery Distributors. So everyone wants your grocery money. Needless to say, the industry is highly competitive.

Jennery knows the supermarket industry well and explained to me the sophisticated distribution system that keeps our cities fed. The average grocery store stocks between thirty thousand and forty thousand products, he said. To ensure that food is always on supermarket shelves requires a supply chain that crosses many borders and is so complex it necessitates a military-style command and control operation.

The supermarket food chain doesn't start in the farmer's field and travel directly to the store. Rather, it begins with negotiations between the chain's buyers, who decide what products will be featured on the store shelves, and the food company's sales representatives, who lobby the supermarkets to sell as many of their products as possible. That's in addition to a myriad of other suppliers. To stock one supermarket, a single retailer may have to deal with fifteen thousand different suppliers, who sell everything from lettuce to beef to breakfast cereal. Once a deal has been made between the two companies and a particular product has been ordered, the product must pass through the supermarket chain's distribution centre, a giant building that would normally be called a warehouse if the product spent any time there. However, it costs money to warehouse products, so the food doesn't remain there for long before being sent on to the store where it is shelved. The supermarket similarly doesn't warehouse food. Instead, it tries to stock only the amount of product it can sell within a few days. As soon as a box of cereal or a bag of milk is scanned at the cash register, the information is uploaded into a database and analyzed by the grocer to ensure there will be enough cereal or milk for the next person who walks into the store.

This is the supermarket's adaptation of the car industry's just-in-time production—in the grocery world, it's called just-in-time replenishment. The logistics are staggering. Suppliers shipping to the distribution centre are given precise delivery appointments, and their trucks must arrive at the specified loading station at the specified time so the food can be repacked and sent on to the stores that need the stock before the product sells out. This means that an average store receives between three and five deliveries a day to maintain its stock, said Jennery. The chains do keep what's called a safety stock in the distribution centre—three days' worth of perishable produce, eight to nine days of frozen foods and fourteen days' worth of dry goods. But other than those stocks, the food that most of us in the city rely on to feed ourselves is on its way here from somewhere far away. Our system is in constant motion.

The supermarket's supply chain is the antithesis of a local food system, and supermarkets are often criticized for selling romaine imported from Mexico at the same time nearby farmers are harvesting heads of romaine. But from a business perspective, said Jennery, it's costly to deal with small producers. "As a retailer, you want to keep costs down—as low as possible plus minimum overhead. Consequently, you can deal with one person for all your lettuce needs."

Increasingly, though, consumers are no longer satisfied with the supermarket's long-distance foods. The Toronto-based organization Local

Food Plus found that, between 2007 and 2008, interest in buying sustainable, local food rose 92 percent. It seems the big food corporations have taken note. Loblaw is stocking more Canadian food and launched a "grown close to home" advertising campaign featuring Canadian farmers in different provinces. In its stores, the chain set up displays reminiscent of farmers' markets. According to Mike Venton, senior vice-president of produce at Loblaw, in 2008, the first year they featured a larger amount of Canadian vegetables, their produce sales rose 12 percent.

Hellmann's Mayonnaise, which is owned by Unilever, produced a video, which it posted on YouTube in 2009, highlighting Canada's diminishing food security in light of the rise in imported foods and the disappearing Canadian family farm. "In a fifteen-year period, our food imports rose 160 percent while our population rose only 15 percent," says the video's stern female narrator. "In 2007, Nova Scotia produced half as many blueberries it did just four years earlier. If this continues . . . many of our small family farms struggle to stay afloat while our grocery dollars end up in other countries." The video sounds like something produced by a food-security coalition, not a multinational corporation, and it remains to be seen whether attempts to gain credibility in the eyes of those concerned about where their food comes from will work—on YouTube, someone has tagged the video "funny propagandas."

Already a backlash against national supermarket chains has begun. In July of 2009, ten Ontario grocers abandoned their Sobeys affiliation so they could meet their customers' demand for local meats. Sobeys company policy, which stated that all meat sold in their stores be processed at a federally (versus provincially) inspected processor, had prevented the grocers from buying meat from nearby farmers. The stores created the Hometown Grocers Co-op so they could source fresh chicken, beef and pork from their neighbours.

Yet while farmers' markets may be busy, and community-supported agriculture plans and box programs are on the rise, these alternative food-sale models represent only 4 percent of the market share, according to Local Food Plus. The mainstream food-distribution system is massive, complex and efficient. Any alternative will have to grapple with these facts.

I can't help but wonder whether the size of our population and the complexity of our society limit the possibility of local food in Canada today. Is this long-distance food chain the only way to supply the city? Or *could* a local food economy feed everybody in a densely populated area?

.

Harriet Friedmann, a professor of sociology and fellow of the Centre for International Studies at the University of Toronto, has spent her long career studying food systems. She made her mark on the field in the 1980s, when she and a colleague, Philip McMichael at Cornell University, coined the term "food regimes" to describe a way of examining food from a historical and geopolitical perspective. The concept helps us to understand the relationship between the creation and development of states and the political economy of food; it connects the dots between politics and food production. Friedmann and McMichael identified two food regimes in the last century, the first linked to the expansion of the British empire. This food regime, dating from 1870 to 1914, was characterized by a new system that sourced cheap food from the colonies—sugar and tea from the tropics, wheat from Canada, animal products from Argentina and New Zealand—for Britain's urban population, which was growing rapidly during industrialization. The second food regime took place after the Second World War and saw mass production of foods by large corporations for mass consumption.

According to the theory, during every food regime, there is conflict between actors (such as farmers and food processors) as they compete for control of the food system. Academics aren't sure whether a third food regime has stabilized yet. It seems, however, that there are two possible futures, explained Friedmann. On the one hand, there exists a global food system controlled primarily by supermarkets, and on the other, a regionally organized and diverse system seems to be taking shape.

Friedmann's opinions on how to organize the food system are sought by people around the world. She is part of the UN-led International Expert Assessment of Agricultural Knowledge, Science, and Technology and sits on the Scientific Committee of the Observatory of World Agriculture led by the French government research institute International Cooperation Centre for Agronomic Research for Development. Her office is on campus at the Munk Centre for International Studies, an old red stone building that was built long before there was such a thing as the complex transnational food system of today. Friedmann is hopeful that a new system, one that is sustainable and local, is in the making; however, when I asked her to explain to me how it could function, she shook her head. "The truth is we don't know," she said. "We don't know how much can be done and what way. There are lots of possibilities one can imagine.

"We have no history or evolutionary experience about how to do local under these circumstances. For the first time in human history, the majority of us live in cities. Cities were built on the most fertile land. And now we've paved that over. You build suburb developments where the farms used to be. There are more people and there is less food because the farmland isn't there. We thought we'd solved all that because we could source our food from other parts of the world. Now we know that the long-distance food system is not sustainable.

"The resilience of the biosphere as a whole—all the forest that was around, the waterways that were so big, the oceans that were abundant—people thought they could absorb all the damage that the industrial system created. That's not true anymore."

Friedmann holds that we are thirty-odd years into this period of flux. It is too early to tell what the new system will look like in the end, but if we look to Toronto today, we can see the early signs of a new way of bringing food into the city.

•

During the summer of 2007 in Toronto, it seemed that every week a new farmers' market opened shop. In downtown parks, suburban churchyards and even mall parking lots, farmers started selling their goods to strong crowds. It was a sudden and popular return to the kinds of open-air markets that helped to feed early Canadian cities. An artist's rendition of the Bonsecours Market in Montreal at the end of the nineteenth century depicts vendors, likely farmers, selling produce from wooden carts. It is a rainy day, and the men selling the food are holding umbrellas over their heads and watching women with shopping baskets walk by. Another picture sketches the apple stalls, hundreds of wide barrels filled with fruit. A drawing of the upper-town market in Quebec City, completed around the same time, shows a winter scene. Freshly slaughtered geese and pheasants dangle by their feet from a pole at one stall; there's a wooden box of some large round vegetable, maybe squash, at another. To one side, a woman chooses from a dozen fish laid out on a makeshift table. These snapshots of life at the farmers' market don't look that different from a market you would see today, minus the petticoats. It's amazing to think how much the world has changed in the 150 years since this artwork was created, and yet a farmers' market is still recognizable as a farmers' market.

There are more than five hundred farmers' markets in Canada today. Toronto alone had more than two dozen in 2009. In 2000 in British Columbia, there were twenty markets; in 2009 there were seventy. According to Farmers' Markets Canada, sales at Canadian markets total a whopping $1.03 billion a year and counting. They are the second most frequented destination for food purchases after the big-box grocery stores among the group of people they questioned. In Calgary, the farmers' market is the largest-grossing retailer in the city.

To accommodate the demand for fresh local foods in cities, regional governments are investing in large civic developments. A new building in downtown Saskatoon houses a year-round market, and in Halifax, an ultramodern complex overlooking the ocean is being built to accommodate the more than ten thousand people who, every Saturday morning, visit the current market that is located in a warren of rooms in an old building downtown. The Halifax market is Canada's oldest—the King of England proclaimed it a market in 1750, one year after Halifax itself was founded. The new market will be massive, and open all week. The latest in green technologies will heat and cool the building, and it will act as a focal point for the many tourists who visit the city; a dock for cruise ships has been incorporated into the design.

Despite their growing popularity, these totems to local agriculture will likely not be the only place people get their food in the city of the future. Although many people enjoy shopping this way, farmers' markets aren't the simple answer to supplying the modern-day city with fresh, local food. The reason for this is technical. Farmers themselves don't have the capacity to move and process the vast quantities of food consumed in urban areas. Many farmers don't even like to go to the markets, and even if they do, it can be a logistical nightmare to harvest the food in time—but not too early, so that it's still fresh—then pack it into trucks and drive to the city with enough time to spare to set up the tables before the customers arrive. All these hours spent away from the fields means that there is work to catch up on when they get back. Many farmers I spoke to while researching this book described their gruelling schedules. Some sleep only a few hours the night before market day. Some spend Sundays making up for the work that was neglected while they were in the city the day before. And while many of them enjoy socializing at the market, not everybody who farms is suited to marketing their own produce and chatting with the folks who buy their food.

That said, the rise in farmers' markets in recent years has been good for farmers. "It's making a huge difference for some farms. There are lots of farmers that make over $1,000 a day in sales at farmers' markets," said

Brent Warner, executive director of Farmers' Markets Canada. He said the markets keep many farms in business and help encourage younger farmers to get into the field. "It's an incubator for new farmers too. New farmers who don't have infrastructure can simply harvest it, load it, truck it and sell it. Young people who want to get into farming can do it without a large amount of capital." Farmers' Markets Canada found that farmers make on average about a third of their income selling at the market. And the larger community benefits from economic spinoffs because the farmers who attend markets hire on average between one and five employees.

Nevertheless, the big food is happening elsewhere. But some people are working to change this too.

. . .

I first met Lori Stahlbrand a number of years ago, before I understood the connection between our food system and climate change. In fact, it was she whom I interviewed when I was investigating that pink-iced Chinese cookie. Stahlbrand has been trailblazing in this area for years. She is among a small group of people who were talking about a localized food system before most of us had even caught on to the benefits of organics, let alone local. A former CBC journalist (she hosted a current affairs show and read the news on the Toronto airwaves during the 1980s and '90s), Stahlbrand left the profession to work on food issues and rethink the way we get food from the farmers' fields to our plates. More than a decade later, she is the president of Local Food Plus, or LFP, which is making huge progress in figuring out ways to create new supply chains to link local farmers with the millions of people who live in Toronto.

Stahlbrand is a tall woman with blond highlights who looks you straight in the eye while she talks. She and her former business partner, Mike Schreiner, built LFP from scratch with a patchwork of grants. Their goal was to help foster a local food system by linking farmers with institutions that buy food in a city, such as hospitals, universities and

corporate cafeterias—the numerous institutions that rely on global supply chains to procure their food. They created their own LFP certification
to brand food as being local and sustainable.

It just so happened that at the same time LFP was starting up,
Stahlbrand was teaching a course at the University of Toronto's New
College, where, coincidentally, the cafeteria's food services contract was
about to expire. One day, Stahlbrand chatted with the college principal
about her ideas for fostering a local and sustainable food system, and
he immediately became interested. One thing led to another and, soon
enough, her new organization was collaborating with the university to
ensure that a minimum amount of local food would be served on campus.
LFP drafted a request for proposals for the new contract that required
the company that would take over the job of feeding tens of thousands
of students on campus to source a specified percentage of the food they
served from Ontario farms. It was a pretty radical idea at the time, with
potentially mind-numbing implications because of the number of people
it would involve. "University of Toronto is like working with a city," said
Stahlbrand. "It's the largest university in North America. There are seventy thousand students. And there are all sorts of different foods available."

The farm-to-school movement in the United States discovered the
power of institutions in building a new food system in the 1990s. The
United States, unlike Canada, has a national school lunch program,
funded by the federal government, that provides a free or subsidized lunch
to about 30 million children a day. In the mid-1990s, Robert Gottleib was
a professor of urban and environmental policy at Occidental College in
Los Angeles. His children were enrolled in public school in the area, and
he was troubled that they were being served what amounted to a daily
dose of junk food when so much fresh and nutritious food was available
nearby. So he approached the food services director at the school and
suggested they buy fresh foods from the Santa Monica farmers' market
rather than frozen fish sticks and fries imported from who knows where.

What started as a pilot project in 1996 in California is now a nation-wide success story, with almost nine thousand schools participating in forty states. The farm-to-school movement has received a lot of support in part because of the role it plays in fighting the much publicized child-hood obesity epidemic. Feeding kids healthy foods is an easy sell. Initially, it was individual farmers who were supplying the food to schools. But demand has been so high that a new player in the food industry, the food service sector, is now participating. And the success of these regional dis-tribution systems has piqued the interest of those in government. There are now state farm-to-school coordinators whose job it is to help set up these distribution routes for food. As well, the focus on institutions has spread to other sectors, like daycares and hospitals. Preschools provide the next challenge. "The earlier you begin trying to change food hab-its, the better," said Anupama Joshi, co-director of the National Farm to School Program.

The idea has also taken off at the college level. In the United States, approximately 150 post-secondary institutions, including Yale, the University of Texas, Princeton and Harvard, now have farm-to-college programs that buy a combination of vegetables, fruits and meat from farmers at most about three hundred kilometres away. Some food service corporations that operate school cafeterias, like Bon Appétit Management and Parkhurst Dining Services, have started to locally source some of the food they serve. Considering these corporate food services are a multi-billion-dollar, transnational industry that is represented on every single continent of the globe, to shift this industry's focus to supporting local food networks would be a major change.

·

Local Food Plus started their work on the University of Toronto campus, but their plans go further than just the university. Bringing this large institution into the city's regional food economy was their first triumph.

Stahlbrand wants her organization to do even more to assemble a functioning regional food system. LFP plans to continue their work with institutions like hospitals, schools and municipalities to involve as many people as possible in the local food economy.

The LFP branding system has helped to inform the rest of us who don't eat in cafeterias and institutions. At a few independent grocery stores in Toronto, you can find products such as yogurt, canned tomatoes and lettuce labelled with their green-and-white LFP logo. These products must meet specific criteria set out by LFP. To be certified as sustainable, a farmer must practise ecologically sound methods, including trying to eliminate pesticides; avoiding the use of antibiotics for livestock and treating animals humanely; protecting soil and waterways; and working to minimize the farm's carbon footprint. Sustainability standards, such as water conservation, recycling programs and reductions in packaging, are applied to food processors too. When shoppers buy LFP-approved products, they know that they are getting something that is local as well as environmentally friendly. Local food producers who display the logo on their products are able to differentiate their product from the many others on the supermarket shelves and possibly gain a little more market share. And retailers competing for those food dollars can offer something different too. For example, after learning of the pesticide load of the average peach, I stopped buying the fruit unless it was organic—but finding an organic Ontario peach is not easy. Then one day I spotted LFP-certified peaches for sale at an independent grocery store. I was so happy that I bought three large baskets and ended up freezing stewed peaches to eat during the winter.

By working simultaneously at all these different levels of the supply chain, Local Food Plus is building a strong and diverse market for local foods that is more likely to support a wide range of regional food growers and processors. And they are using their clout to ensure that the farmers are practising sustainable agriculture. It's a total system overhaul. Already more than a hundred farms are certified. Not only is their food served at the university but it is available to wholesalers at the Ontario Food Terminal and served in restaurants too. They've had an enormous impact and they plan to expand their work into other provinces, likely Quebec and British Columbia.

Stahlbrand acknowledges that they have a long way to go. "It's not going to happen overnight. Food supply chains are all global now, and the cost of transportation has been so low that how far it's transported or how many times it's transported hasn't mattered." And yet she's hopeful. Because everyone has to eat every day, the potential for change is huge. "In this sense, it is empowering for people that they can make choices. You eat three times a day. If you didn't make that choice at lunch, you can at dinner." Slowly, slowly, a local food system is being developed.

. . .

If efforts like those of LFP are indicative of a new food regime, then, as the theory goes, all major change comes with tension as actors duke it out for control of the food system. While Stahlbrand and LFP work to build a regional system, critics claim that what they are trying to create can never function in a place like Toronto. They say that locally produced food is too costly and that a regional system will make it difficult for people of all income groups to access food. Another fear is that the public's diverse tastes will not be satisfied by what we can produce in Ontario. Indeed, price and diversity of food represent two large hurdles to overcome when building a sustainable and local food system. How *do* you ensure that food grown near the city is affordable to everyone? And how do you satisfy a city where people are accustomed to eating croissants for breakfast, sushi for lunch and eggplant curry for dinner? These issues, however, also have been raised by people involved in the local food movement, and efforts are being made to address them.

I am often a food tourist in my own city. In Mississauga, I like to drop by a restaurant in an industrial area where they make pita from scratch and bake it in a wood-burning oven. The fresh bread complements perfectly the grilled chicken and hummus. In Thorncliffe Park, I must stop at the Indian sweet shop—across the way from my favourite Afghan kebab house—to pick up some habshi halwa. I can't resist the taste of milk that has been boiled with sugar and cardamom and turned into a soft cake. Then I stop in at Ichbal's, a South Asian grocery store, to buy the ingredients for my favourite Indian snack, pani poori, those crispy gram flour shells filled with potato, chickpeas and chutney. The diversity of what we eat here is fantastic.

And yet, it is possible to make many of these foods with locally produced ingredients, and we are able to grow some of this produce here; in this way, we can create a local food system that caters to myriad cuisines. The African Food Basket, one of Toronto's largest urban-agriculture projects, whose volunteers tend six gardens in the north end of the city, grows leafy greens that are popular in the Caribbean, like callaloo, to appeal to local tastes. Farms in Canada grow different kinds of mushrooms, including Asian ones. We produce foods such as couscous, chickpea flour and paneer, and we bake naan in factories for mass distribution.

When it comes to foods like avocado, in a healthy and sustainable local food system, guacamole needn't be wiped from the menu. Though it's unlikely that we'll ever grow avocados here, even in the best greenhouses, there's no reason we can't enjoy some tropical produce. If a good portion of our food is produced nearby in a sustainable way, then it should be all right to eat some avocados grown sustainably elsewhere. An avocado will have a higher food-miles count than a local apple, but not all food miles are created equal. An avocado transported by cargo ship or train will have less of a carbon footprint, for example, than one flown here.

Indeed, some people working to build local food systems are thinking creatively about transport solutions. Wayne Roberts, coordinator of the Toronto Food Policy Council, suggested we might sail tropical food like fair-trade coffee and tea around the globe. James E. McWilliams, an associate professor of history at Texas State University and the author of the book *Just Food*, which criticized the locavore movement, argues that by ruling out imports, we shut out innovation and the possibility of creating clean technology to minimize the impact of long-distance imports. If we are no longer flying snow peas from China and are growing them here instead, there should be room for some avocados.

Those who support a global industrial food system often argue that we *need* the cheap food produced by this system so everybody can eat; Canadians produce expensive food while Mexicans, for example, make it more cheaply. They have a point. Labour, as well as land and other agricultural inputs, costs more in Canada. Also, when food is produced with care for the environment, as is the case on LFP-certified farms, it can be more expensive because the cost of production is higher. When an organic farmer lets a field lie fallow to improve its fertility rather than pumping it with chemical fertilizer, income from that field is temporarily lost; the environmental costs are internalized. When LFP compares the cost of the foods they certify with those of the average products you buy at the grocery store, they find that their prices are about 10 percent higher; milk and meat can cost double the price of conventional products.

However, the local-food movement is committed to creating a new system for all people of all income levels, both here in Canada and in less developed countries in the global south. In Toronto, groups like The Stop Community Food Centre, which is founded on the belief that food is a basic human right, are working to improve access to nutritious food and to support a sustainable regional food system. The Stop operates a three-thousand-square-foot greenhouse as well as community gardens and composts, and runs a food bank, a farmers' market and programs designed to educate people about eating well. In lower-income neighbourhoods, volunteers with the organization sell at affordable prices fruits and vegetables they purchase directly from farmers at the Ontario Food Terminal.

Nick Saul, The Stop's executive director, is aware of the higher cost of vegetables at the farmers' market they run in a refurbished street-car building called the Wychwood Barns, located in an upper-income neighbourhood in the city's midtown. So he and his colleagues have created an ingenious program to ensure that the people they serve who can't afford to pay these prices can still access this good food. The Stop solicits cash donations from the public that they use to pay a nearby farmer to grow organic vegetables for the centre; it's a group take on community-supported agriculture. They have also partnered with the farmer and Fiesta Farms, an independent grocer, so that when someone purchases, say, beets at this store, 10 percent of the money goes into a fund to pay the organic farmer to grow more vegetables for The Stop. "That's a very entrepreneurial way to get farmers to grow ecologically," said Saul. The organization is using their purchasing power to support sustainable agriculture while at the same time ensuring that these healthy foods are accessible to people who can't afford to shop at the farmers' markets. "If everyone has access to the best food out there—that's sustainable food—then our city will be a better place," he said.

Debbie Field, executive director of FoodShare in Toronto, also wants to ensure that in building a local food system, we include those who don't have a lot of money to spend on food. FoodShare is a Toronto non-profit that works at the grassroots level to build a food system that is both just and environmentally sustainable. They run a program for every link in the food chain, from the growing (they oversee an urban farm on the grounds of the Centre for Addiction and Mental Health that produces vegetables for sale at a farmers' market), to the processing (they offer small food-business start-ups access to industrial kitchens), to distribution (their Good Food Box program provides fresh fruits and vegetables to people of all economic backgrounds who subscribe).

"For me, everything is about fresh fruit and vegetables," Field said. "I believe in the revolutionary power of fresh fruit and vegetables to change the world. But in our desire to help farmers we are trying to push the price of food up. We believe farmers have not got a good deal. Sometimes when I go to a farmers' market, I don't feel comfortable with the prices because they are so out of whack with the food system."

The pressing question for Field is how to ensure that you don't end up with a two-tiered food system—one where high-quality foods are available to those who can afford their boutique prices and another where mass-produced industrial foods feed the less prosperous. She sees a role for government in helping to make food accessible to all citizens. She also believes that urban agriculture is part of the solution to making local food accessible to everyone. "The whole city of Toronto is on grade A agricultural land. I don't think it is unreasonable to think we can grow a quarter of our vegetables. And some of our fruit too." Her reasoning is that when there is more supply, prices will come down. "I don't think any of us know how much food we can grow in Toronto."

. . .

For all my questioning and interviewing and attempts to figure out what a local foodshed would look like for a city the size of Toronto, I still could not quite visualize a working system that could feed the millions. Farmers' markets alone will not supply us with enough food, and the supermarkets are inextricably embedded in the global supply chain. The food terminal helps to bring in local produce, but a lot of the food eaten in the city doesn't pass through this central market. I decided I needed a vision for the city. So, once more, I called Harriet Friedmann, as she is one of the global experts on food systems. I asked her to imagine Toronto as it could be. She indulged me with her dreams for the future.

"We'd have changes in energy and transportation," she started to muse. "Some of the paved area could be gardens. We could pay people to garden or farm. Or they could lease the land. We'd have a lot more urban gardening of fresh produce. In suburban spaces, we'd be producing a lot more of our fresh fruit and vegetables too. We'd be experimenting with greenhouses. We'd have solar systems for water. We don't want to be digging up soil on farms and bringing it in from the country, so we'd have centralized composting. Fish in tanks—there are just so many things. The whole city would be less segregated from the ecosystem in which we live. We are so distant from everything in our food system. When people get contact with it, they feel good, they are attracted to it."

She also stressed that an important component of such a system would be to pay farmers in the country for their role as environmental stewards. Farmers, in addition to producing food, provide society with ecological goods and services, she pointed out. Farmers take care of waterways, they protect wildlife habitat such as wetlands and forests, they nurture the soil, and they preserve both nature and our food-growing abilities for future generations. On Prince Edward Island, as well as in Norfolk County in Ontario, there exists an innovative initiative called the Alternative Land Use Services program to compensate farmers for their important societal role. In P.E.I., farmers enrolled in ALUS are paid by the hectare to remove their land from production as well as to protect waterways from livestock that can damage habitat and pollute water. The goal is to stop erosion and promote soil conservation by protecting marginal lands such as sloped fields. In Norfolk County, farmers are remunerated for planting deep-rooting native grasses on sensitive lands that help to sequester carbon; they can harvest the grass to feed to their cattle instead of corn. They are also planting their hedgerows with flowers attractive to the bees and insects that are needed to pollinate the crops. These programs work to lower the cost of ecologically produced food because when farmers are paid for protecting the environment, they do not bear the economic burden of their actions. Another benefit of paying farmers for their environmental stewardship, said Friedmann, is that they are no longer dependent on the price they can get for the food they grow. "We have to detach the farmers' income from the price of food. Since farmers are managing the land, the water, in certain ways, the air, why don't we acknowledge this?" she said.

In Friedmann's system, the food these farmers grow would be sold in nearby cities, in neighbourhood farmers' markets but also in little shops and greengrocers dotted throughout the city's neighbourhoods. "We need to increase the markets for farmers bringing in healthy foods. We design a system and we continue redesigning it as we see it. If there's a problem, then we fix it. The food system would be much more integrated into our lives."

She believes that the farmers' markets, the CSAs, the box programs, the many different ways people are coming up with to distribute local food, are the beginning of a new system. The first signs of an alternative. She likens these to the weeds that come in after a forest is clear-cut. "They create conditions for new plants and animals to come in and a new ecosystem to form," she said. "That would be the vision for a new food system. To come together to produce something quite new."

The next time I go to the farmers' market, I think of Harriet's metaphor. I imagine the people I see are the first signs of a new way, that one day soon we will be able to feed cities teeming with people with a local food system that doesn't use more resources than it produces.

CHAPTER SEVEN

LA RÉVOLUTION DU FROMAGE

Gastronomy in Quebec

The milk from the Bolduc family cows travels through a thirty-metre-long pipe suspended four metres in the air, stretching from their barn to the *fromagerie*. The pipe is insulated to ensure the liquid remains exactly the same temperature as it was when it left the cow. It flows into the make-vat, where begins the process of crafting a cheese they call Alfred Le Fermier, or Alfred the farmer. It's my favourite Quebec cheese: sharp yet creamy, firm but not hard, and salty yet not too salty. When you eat it, the soft taste of the flowers and the grasses that grow in the fields where the Bolduc family cows graze spreads across your tongue. Heaven. Please pass some bread and wine.

Twice a week the folks at the Fromagerie La Station carry out the meticulous process of moving the milk from the cows' udders into the dairy. The cows' teats are cleaned, the milking machine attached carefully and then the liquid pumped. It has to be a meticulous process because here, they don't pasteurize the milk before they make the cheese. For Alfred Le Fermier to taste like Alfred Le Fermier, with the flavour of fresh grass and wild flowers, it must be made from cow-warm raw milk, and so care is taken to ensure that the milk is pure and clean.

Alfred Le Fermier is named after Alfred Bolduc, my host Simon-Pierre's grandfather who bought this land back in 1928. The family has been grazing their cattle on these fields ever since. They are new to cheese making, however, and have been turning the milk into curds to sell only since 2004. Simon-Pierre Bolduc is the head cheese maker, the *directeur d'usine*, head of commercialization and marketing—and he's only twenty-four years old. Simon-Pierre has loopy golden curls and a wide smile. He looks bookish in his wire-rimmed glasses, but he wears the farmer's essential plaid shirt with his khaki pants. When he talks, he gets excited easily and claps his hands together, his smile spreading even further across his face.

It was a beautiful day at the beginning of July when I arrived at the farm, and the sun was shining so brightly I had to squint to see his face. Although he is young, when he speaks he sounds older than he is, wise, almost philosophical. When I asked him to show me how the cheese is made he said, as if he stepped out of the pages of a Michael Pollan book, "We'll start at the beginning. With the fields."

Just beyond the barn, we found the cows grazing. The grass was a deep green, the sky, blue, with white cottony fair-weather cumulus clouds. The cows, wearing the black and white pattern of the Holstein, stopped munching on the grass to look up at us, curious to see what was going on, but quickly lost interest and went back to eating. The cheese making starts here, said Simon motioning to the fields. This idyllic scene is the start of the cycle. His voice rose with excitement, his smile getting bigger. He loves what he does on the farm, loves to steward the milk from the fields all the way to the blocks of cheese they sell in their farm store. "We just have to give them water, shade and pasture and they do it all themselves."

Simon-Pierre says the humans on the farm are merely stewards rather than masters of the cheese-making process because the cows subsist primarily on grass (though their diet is topped up with a bit of nutritional grain so they can sustain two milkings a day without getting too thin).

Cows have four stomachs, and in the first one, the rumen, bacteria digest cellulose, the basic makeup of grass that we humans can't digest. By feeding the cows mostly grass, Simon-Pierre believes he is letting the natural processes perfected through evolution take place with little human interference.[16] In the summer the cows are put to pasture, and in the winter, Simon-Pierre's younger brother Vincent, who takes care of them, feeds them organic hay made up of dried alfalfa and clover that he's sowed, cut and baled in the family's fields.

"This is the most simple. One should not complicate things," said Simon-Pierre. And because the cows subsist primarily on grass, their milk—and thus their cheese—reflects the seasonal changes of nature. "There is more flavour in the summer. The milk smells different. It's more dense. In the winter, it's creamier. We make good cheeses in the summer, because there's more flavour. But the best cheese of the year is in September and October. C'est les merveilles." He sighed. "It tastes like grass on a brisk day, with lots of sun. It's the best cheese."

To shape the flavour of their cheese, the Bolducs select certain grasses over others. Simon-Pierre and Vincent work together to figure out which kinds they feel bring out the flavours they are looking for. Alfalfa, for example, gives the cheese a bitter taste, whereas red and white clover offer a good flavour. But yellow sweet clover and timothy, these are the foundations for a great-tasting cheese. "From the blade of grass to the block of cheese, this is what I tell my clients," said Simon-Pierre.

And then he tells me something that radically alters my understanding of local food. I know "local" to mean the food we eat that comes from the soil around here, food that is raised in our midst, a product of this place. I also know to include preserving knowledge of food preparation as an integral part of a local food system. Simon-Pierre adds local bacteria to this list. When he makes his cheese here, he wants it to be flavoured by these local micro-organisms. "If you add industrial bacteria, you lose the terroir. The colour, the taste, the texture is different," he said. Rather than using only cheese culture, a powder that cheese makers buy through the mail and add to their milk to begin the maturation process, the Bolducs want to use the flora that occur naturally on the farm. One day, they hope to cut out these purchased cheese cultures completely.

The bacteria Simon-Pierre wants to flavour his cheese with are those "in Compton, at the Ferme de la Station, owned by the *famille* Bolduc, on this day, at this altitude. The weather is such, there are certain plants that grow. The cows lie in the fields and the bacteria of the plants get into the milk. This is the definition of raw-milk cheese." And the appreciation of these local bacteria is culture.

. . .

Without wading into the politics of *la société distincte*, I will posit that Quebec culture is decidedly different from other regional cultures in Canada. This is largely because, in Quebec, there exists something called *la patrimoine gastronomique*, loosely translated as gastronomical heritage that is rooted in patriotism. "It's localism," explained Lara Rabinovitch, the managing editor of the McGill University e-journal of Canadian food culture, *Cuizine*, and a PhD candidate at New York University. "An intense devotion to the local product. Cultural patriotism through food. It's national identity through consumption." *Patrimoine gastronomique* includes an understanding of terroir, the notion that the taste of a food is affected by a region's soil, its climate, its landscape, its hours of sunlight— that the place where food is made is inextricably linked to what it is. And this is a key component of a local food system.

In Quebec today, the concept of terroir, one that is only now catching on in other parts of the country, is thriving. In the last two decades, small artisan food producers have started to experiment successfully in parts of the province such as the Eastern Townships and the Charlevoix, an area north of Quebec City bordering the Saint Lawrence. Just as in France, where specialties have evolved based on which crops and livestock do best in a certain geographic area, people in Quebec's various regions are creating their own foods, shaped by their landscape and climate. Today, there is cheese making in all regions. In the Charlevoix, they make blue, camembert, migneron and cheddar. Les Îles-de-la-Madeleine, a remote archipelago of islands in the Gulf of Saint Lawrence, are known for Pied-de-Vent, while the Isle-aux-Grues, another group of islands in the middle of the Saint Lawrence east of Quebec City, is known for Riopelle and Mi-Carême made with milk taken from cows that graze on the *foins de la batture,* the sea grasses in the tidal lands. There is also cheddar in Lac-Saint-Jean, as well as in the Eastern Townships, where Simon-Pierre farms. The way a culture of eating has fostered a cheese revival across the province shows us how the general public can help to build a thriving local food system.

Quebec's *patrimoine gastronomique* has been simmering for centuries, ever since the first colonists landed in what was then home to the First Nations people. The early settlers arrived with their French food culture, but were ill equipped to feed themselves during the long and harsh North American winter. Without the help of the Native people who taught the newcomers how to prepare food from the wilderness, the Europeans would not have survived. The First Nations people shared with them their knowledge of both wild foods and indigenous crops their ancestors had domesticated, such as corn and sunflowers, and a multicoloured squash called the Iroquois pumpkin, which early texts reveal was of particular interest to the colonists. The Europeans incorporated these indigenous foods into their diets, and this initial mixing of food cultures eventually led to a cuisine particular to Quebec.

The early cookbooks in the province reveal the beginnings of this syncretic cuisine—a style that amounts to what we would call fusion today. Some dishes would blend ingredients from two traditions. For example, Samuel de Champlain, the founder of Quebec City who arrived in North America in the seventeenth century, is said to have been the first person to plant lettuce from Europe on this continent; by the eighteenth century, people were dressing their salads in bear oil. The successive generations, bolstered in number by new immigrants, placed a high value on food. In Quebec City, where in 1755 there were only 7,200 residents, 80 of them were innkeepers, whose focus was preparing foods in the early restaurants of the colony. These men (the French cooking trades were dominated by men) were mostly from France. There they would likely have trained as bakers, pastry chefs and cooks, bringing their *savoir-faire* across the ocean to feed a new population. During this period, an entire industry devoted to food preparation was booming at the local *traiteur*—which translates as caterer, the place where you'd go to buy prepared foods such as sausages, charcuterie, tarts, brioches, larded roasts, venison, beef ribs *bonne femme* and more that the urban wealthy would bring home to eat.

By the nineteenth century, French-Canadian cuisine freely incorporated foods from Europe, such as olive oil and capers, that could be imported by ship. These were added to dishes made with native ingredients, including passenger pigeon, eel from the Saint Lawrence and beaver tail. In this way, they created a typically North American cuisine, officially identified in the 1840s with the publication of a popular cookbook called *La Cuisinière Canadienne*. This was the foundation of the *patrimoine gastronomique*, the cultural heritage linked to the taste of place, which would, hundreds of years later, shape a whole new generation of cheese makers and eaters.

To this day, the past continues to influence the Quebec palate, said Laurier Turgeon, a professor of history and ethnology at Laval University. "The two go together. There is what was inherited from the indigenous people—maple syrup, wild plants like fiddleheads. Then there is the European, specifically French, heritage. It's all linked to history and geography. But there is also a desire today, to distinguish contemporary Quebec cuisine from France, to have a gastronomy that is original." When it comes to cheese, this means that you will find different ones in

Quebec than you will in France, cheeses that reflect the distinct geography and history of the province.

•

Quebeckers have a long history of making cheese. As soon as the beginnings of a colony took root in the years after the Europeans arrived, the settlers sought a way to preserve milk. Cheese was likely one of the first foods made here, said Patrick Tirard-Collet, a professor at the Institut de technologie agroalimentaire in Sainte-Hyacinthe. Tirard-Collet has a passion for the history of cheese making in the province and has dug through his school's archives searching for the story of how it became an important part of the diet in New France. Already in the 1620s, Samuel de Champlain had a herd of cattle—it is said that this farm, where they kept "70 *bêtes à cornes*," was the first dairy farm in North America. The cows there were bred to adapt to the harsh climate. This genetic stock would eventually be called the Canadian breed. The milk they produced had a very high butterfat content, and from the beginning, said Tirard-Collet, it was likely used to make cheese.

The earliest records of cheese making in the province, however, are from the Lord of Beauport, Robert Giffard, who in 1643 governed a swath of land awarded to him by the King of France. He requested a food-render— that is, cheese as rent from the settler-farmers who were working the land under his purview, a practice that was common in Europe. Cheese making quickly became part of life, and by the end of the seventeenth century on Île d'Orléans, upriver from Quebec City, ten families were producing a ripened cheese the island would become known for. The most famous cheese-making family was the Aubins, who passed their secret recipe from mother to daughter, generation after generation, as a way of preserving the cheese for centuries. Sadly, this tradition ended when they tried to modernize their production in the 1980s and their cheese cultures, the local flora that flavoured the cheese, didn't survive the new sanitation efforts at the dairy. Since the cheese no longer tasted the same, the family stopped producing it.

For most of Quebec history, however, cheese was primarily something made at home on the farm, by the women. It was called a *faisselle*, a quick cheese prepared in a farm kitchen that is creamy and soft, much like a camembert. To make their cheeses, the women would take the enzyme rennet from a calf's stomach and use it to coagulate the milk, giving it the consistency of jello. They would then put the gelatinous mixture in a ceramic mould and leave it to sit for ten hours, salting it and turning it to ensure that the whey drained off, leaving a firmer cheese behind. Next, they would remove the cheese from the ceramic and leave it to age on a bed of straw. Usually, they would keep the cheese somewhere high up in the kitchen, often above the wood stove, where the smoke and the heat would protect it from flies. These were very rustic cheeses, based on recipes likely to have travelled with the people who came from France. Because they were soft, they didn't keep for a long time and weren't very well suited to the North American climate, with winters that required people to preserve foods for long periods.

At the same time the women were preparing *faisselle* on the farm, another kind of cheese making was taking place in the province's abbeys. In Oka and later at the Benedictine monastery at Saint-Benoît-du-Lac in the Eastern Townships, monks who were supposed to live by the work of their own hands were turning milk into curds to sell to the public. These were the antitheses of the quick and easy *faisselle*. While the farm wife, often mother to many children, had to make her cheese quickly so she could get back to sewing the clothes, doing the laundry, cooking the meals, tending the fire, chopping wood and the countless other tasks involved in subsistence farming, the monk was required by his vocation to *fill* his time. As they still say at Saint-Benoît-du-Lac, where the monks run a farm, grow apples to press into cider and have made cheese since 1943: "Idleness is the enemy of the soul." The monastery cheese is therefore a more labour-intensive product. Oka, which is a type of Port-Salut, brought to Canada from Brittany by Trappist monks in the nineteenth century, was washed with brine by hand. This daily chore develops its thick, orange-coloured rind.

It was with the arrival of the Loyalists from the United States in the nineteenth century that the long-time practice of making cheese on the farm started to disappear. The Loyalists were of British origin and pre-ferred cheddar, a cheese conducive to a factory-style method of produc-tion. They opened the first cheese factories. The cheese makers pooled milk from various farms to turn into cheddar. Some was kept to eat, but most was exported to satisfy a growing British demand for this cheese. These factories quickly grew in number, and by end of the nineteenth century there were more than fifteen hundred cheese factories in Quebec alone. "In that time period, the first French cheeses disappeared," said Tirard-Collet. After that, we don't see them anymore. Cheddar became the only cheese that was made."

Even though cheddar was produced in large batches and in a factory, what they were making in the late 1800s was nevertheless an artisan-style cheese. It was made by hand, largely by men because the job was so physi-cally demanding. But it was an art too. The men would watch the changes to the milk and let the curd tell them when to proceed to the next stage. The wax-coated blocks they crafted became the foundation of the dairy industry in Canada well into the next century as they fed English demand. Quebec was not alone in Canada in producing cheese for the English market. Nova Scotia's Annapolis County was home to the Pioneer cheese factory, which produced 900,000 pounds of cheese in 1871. Cheese fac-tories were also in operation in New Brunswick, Manitoba, Alberta and British Columbia. Ontario had a strong cheese-making industry too; 322 factories in the province were making cheddar for export in 1870. Seven years after this, Canada was producing 60 percent of England's cheese; Quebec alone was responsible for 30 percent of that. And the cheddar was good too. At the 1893 World's Fair in Chicago, Canadian cheddar won all the top prizes.

But these artisanal cheese-making traditions faded from Canadian, as well as Québécois, culture during the latter half of the twentieth century, when the food system was modernized. When large dairy companies like Agropur and Kraft started to make cheese, the small factories were forced to consolidate to compete. The vast majority of these small-time operations disappeared. As the old cheese makers died—the men who'd spent their lives working in the rural factories cutting the curd, men who intimately knew how to turn cow's milk into a cheese that reflected the tastes of the place—the art was lost. In Quebec, and right across the country, little knowledge of how to make cheese the old-fashioned way remained. On the farm and in the city, Quebeckers started to choose Kraft Singles and Cheez Whiz instead of their local products. And the province's *patrimoine gastronomique* was put on hold.

. . .

Some say the artisanal cheese movement has its roots in the sixties, as part of the rise of nationalism that grew out of the Quiet Revolution. Others say it was in the 1980s that a back-to-the-land movement in the province heightened people's interest in rediscovering their culture's food traditions. Regardless when it started, something significant happened, and the zeitgeist of cheese making struck the province. By the mid-1990s, people on a number of farms across the province had started to make cheese by hand, in small batches, from goat, sheep and, a little later, cow's milk. Many of these first producers were city people who had decided to return to the country and try their hand at farming. Often they owned small herds of goats and sheep and needed to do something with their milk, so they tried making cheese. In Quebec, goat's and sheep's milk aren't covered by dairy quotas, the supply management system that regulates the production, marketing and distribution of milk. While farmers with dairy cows had to apply to the dairy board to use their own milk to make cheese, goat and sheep farmers were free to experiment as they wished.

At first the cheeses were uneven. The debutante cheese makers fiddled around with recipes, trying to figure out how to make a good, consistent product. Alain Besré, who is in charge of distribution at the Fromagerie Atwater, was one of the first patrons of these new artisans. Besré runs one of the largest cheese counters in Canada and buys and sells cheeses from around the world. Until the mid-1990s, the Fromagerie Atwater specialized in European cheese, offering their customers such delicacies as Saint-André, Roquefort and Parmigiano-Reggiano. Then suddenly, almost out of nowhere, the farmers arrived with their artisanal cheeses. "Three to four cheese producers came out with cheese at the same time," Besré said. "Nobody talked terroir back then. We thought if we don't buy them, these guys will go nowhere. It became like a mission, you know. The important thing was that they were starting to make cheese." Besré's boss made the decision to support the new industry in Quebec, and Besré was on orders to buy whatever was available. So when the cheese maker would appear with a cheese, the Fromagerie Atwater would pay cash, no matter what the condition of the product. "Making a cheese, it takes many years. You get good batches, mediocre ones. Back then, farmers made cheese and you could see it's farm made." Today, about 40 percent of the cheeses the shop sells are made in Quebec. The appetite in the city for this new cheese is huge.

. . .

Simon-Pierre Bolduc is part of this twenty-first-century cheese-making revolution. At the Fromagerie La Station, his mother started the family's cheese-making story. When I first heard about their dairy in Compton, it was Carole Routhier I was told about, her amazing talent for turning the family's organic milk into the most marvellous cheeses, recipes she conjured up herself. In 1995, Carole saw an ad in the newspaper for a cheese-making course, enrolled in it and was inspired to try what she learned at home. She started with small batches of a hard cheese she would let age in an old broken fridge in the basement; she stuffed its drawers with ice to maintain the right temperature. To start the culture, she used bacteria from yogurt. "It wasn't the best at first. I didn't know what I was doing," she remembered. But she loved the process. She loved to watch her cheeses age. She loved to remove them from the fridge and wash their skins, witness their change in colour. And then slowly the cheese became good—really good. "It was stunning," she said. "That I made them, that I produced this from just milk."

At first the family kept the cheese for themselves and continued to operate as a regular dairy farm, selling their organic milk through the local marketing board, doing what the family had done since their ancestors started to farm. In 2003, they invested in a professional dairy, a laboratory-white building with stainless steel equipment and multiple hand-washing stations that complied with federal standards. They received the requisite permits to make and sell the cheese on the farm, and started the business.

For the next few years, it was a small-scale operation. Then Simon-Pierre returned from agricultural college, where he had studied in the organic dairy program and learned about managing just this kind of operation. When his mom asked him to help with the daily task of washing the rinds, he saw more than rows of cheeses ageing in the cool and humid room they used for ripening and maturation. He saw a shiny future for the family business. Quickly, he took over the operation and expanded it. He went to France to learn more about cheese. He hired some staff, young people who felt as passionately about food as he did. And he made some further renovations to the dairy. The operation today makes 800 kilograms of cheese a week; the revenue supports the entire family.

At the *fromagerie* they now make four kinds of cheese—a raclette suitable for a traditional French wintertime meal of melted cheese and potatoes, the Alfred Le Fermier, and two varieties of what they call Comtomme (the name a play on the town's name and the famous French cheese tomme). They hired a consultant to help develop the recipe for the Comtomme, which is creamy and can be more mild than the Alfred Le Fermier and sells very well. In 2009, at the Canadian Cheese Grand Prix, all four of their cheeses were finalists, the Comtomme and the Alfred Le Fermier winning in their respective categories. Now they have a hard time keeping up with demand.

The Alfred Le Fermier remains their signature product. It's in this cheese that all the flavours of their terroir come out—the sun, the grass, the hay. "I realize this is what I was working on for all those years," said Simon-Pierre's mother of her early experiments with the old fridge in the basement. "It's the cheese that sums up the farm."

. . .

All cheese, no matter if it is made by hand or in a factory, is based on the same principles of curdling milk and draining away the watery stuff, the whey, to leave a substance that will keep longer than fresh milk—and taste good. Cheese makers today still use the same techniques that humans have refined over thousands of years. When the cheese maker, whether in a factory or a farm dairy, adds the rennet and lets the milk coagulate, he is going through the same steps that archaeological finds have shown humans undertaking as long as five thousand years ago.

The difference between industrial and artisanal cheese lies primarily in the way it is made. A true artisanal cheese is prepared in small batches, by hand, whereas industrial cheese making is all mechanized. This doesn't necessarily mean industrial cheese is bad cheese. Some cheeses made in factories do resemble plastic more than they do the delectable dairy product they were named after, like those long skinny blocks of bright orange mild cheddar you find at the grocery store. But Europeans in particular have devised ways to make high-quality cheeses in large quantities. In

France, robots cruise up and down aisles and aisles of ageing cheeses, washing their rinds just as humans would have done, helping to create flavour. This type of cheese is big business. Millions of dollars are invested in trying to replicate the flavour-making chemical compounds that are found in products from the terroir such as Alfred Le Fermier.

And yet no matter how much money is spent trying to capture the *je ne sais quoi* of the artisan, there is something qualitatively different between an industrial cheese and one made by hand. The latter simply looks, feels and tastes like something organic. Cheese making is an art. When the human hand touches the curds, the outcome is never the same. Every batch is different, and depending on the season, the fat and protein content of the milk fluctuates. Industrially made cheeses tend to always have the same colour and texture, whereas in an artisanal cheese, colour, texture, even taste can be unexpected.

When a cheese maker attempts to craft a new cheese, she doesn't follow a recipe. Yes, there are guidelines—you handle the curd differently, depending on the result you like. But it is kind of like writing a new piece of music. There are folk songs and symphonies, tango and rock, different styles to choose from as the songwriter uses the notes and rhythms to compose. What is made from these standard ingredients depends on the artist. It's the same with cheese. To make a camembert-style cheese, you would add penicillin to the milk and then pour the mixture into a mould to age. A blue cheese is often injected with moulds that make those blue and green veins. To produce a hard cheese, such as a cheddar or parmesan, you must cook the milk to firm up the curd. But how each of these will taste depends on more than the sum of its parts.

Perfecting the recipe for a new cheese involves years of fiddling to determine how much salt to use, how best to wash it and what kind of wood plank to age it on. When Quebec cheese maker Luc Mailloux, famous for his fight in the 1990s to legalize raw-milk cheese in Quebec, was starting to develop his products, he said he threw out batch after batch because he didn't feel it was good enough to sell, let alone edible. Such is the art of cheese making.

And yet even when the cheese is brought to market, the cheese maker will still need to make improvements to the taste. This is where the customer played an important role in Quebec's cheese revolution. When the first artisanal cheeses came on the market there, the customers helped to refine the recipes for what is made today—and unwittingly helped to strengthen a local food system. This all took place at one of Montreal's bustling markets.

·

The Atwater Market was overflowing with local produce when I visited in July. Freshly picked fava beans, strawberries, green beans, peas, zucchini and eggplant were displayed on tables around the perimeter of the main building. A Vietnamese farm family asked their young son to explain that they grow and sell Asian vegetables, like long, green eggplants they produce organically on their farm not too far away. There were flowers for sale, and herbs like basil and coriander with a perfume so strong I could smell them from metres away. But the busiest place at the market was the cheese counter at the Fromagerie Atwater, down the stairs at the back of a storefront in the main building, in a small room crammed with tables and open coolers overflowing with pre-packaged cheeses. Behind the counter, a team of cheesemongers, all wearing white aprons and caps, were busy at work, slicing samples for the customers, cutting and weighing big blocks of cheese, wrapping them up as quickly as possible so they could move on to the next person in the snaking line. An incredible sixteen hundred people come into the store to buy cheese every Saturday.

Distribution manager Alain Besré said it was here at the counter where many of the cheeses they still sell today were refined by the people who shop in the store. "The customers love a new product," he said. Every weekend they'd arrive at the market hungry for something new to try.

"Back then, you could say it's farm-made and people would buy it, even if it was crooked," he said. (That's not so easy with today's sophisticated customer base; the cheese has to look *and* taste good now.) They'd take some home and come back the next Saturday with feedback—the cheese didn't melt very well, it was too salty, it developed mould quickly, or it was perfect. This information was transmitted back to the cheese makers, who adjusted their recipes.

At the same time, the customers' knowledge of the cheeses was being shaped by the cheesemonger. Max Dubois, cheesemonger and owner of the Montreal-area L'Échoppe des Fromages, calls what he does taste education. He helps customers to broaden their palate. "Cheese has become the metaphor for our culture," he said. "A metaphor for terroir, for our dream or vision of living in harmony with nature." His role as cheese merchant is that of cultural interpreter, helping to link the farm and the city.

And it is this very flow of ideas that is the basis for a culture of gastronomy. Professor Laurier Turgeon of Laval University, who has spent several years studying the growing local food movement in his province, holds that the *patrimoine gastronomique* often originates in the city where the consumers live. "It's urbanites who consume the products from the terroir. They have a desire to reconnect with the country, to connect with the terroir and to return to the past." This creates a demand for artisanal products, he said. It pushes people to go out into the countryside and buy foods directly from farmers and small-scale producers. And so this culture of gastronomy rooted in a place helps to bolster a developing local food economy.

.

Canada's dairy quota system has kept milk very local in this country. You can't import fresh milk from the United States or Mexico or any other country. However, it is not forbidden to import the industrial milk product that is often listed on the labels of processed foods as modified milk ingredients or milk protein. These show up in all sorts of dairy products, including cheese, ice cream, yogurt—even a jug of pre-made mango lassi they sell at my nearby supermarket. Milk ingredients are a cheap stand-in for fresh milk and thus a ready way for companies to lower their costs. These milk ingredients are made in a factory by passing fresh milk through machines that work like a series of sieves, separating the main cheese-making proteins from the fat, sugar and water. The result is a concentrated-protein liquid that is sprayed into hot air and dried into a powder. These are not a local dairy product, as most modified milk ingredients are imported from New Zealand and Europe.

If you want to eat locally, said Julia Rogers of Cheese Culture, a cheese education and consulting firm in Toronto that offers cheese-tasting courses, she suggests staying away from cheeses made with modified milk ingredients and other processed dairy products, including butter oil, freeze-dried whey and powdered milk. "From a taste-of-place perspective, that's kind of anathema," she said. "It's like your suit. The label says it's made in Italy. But the buttons are from Romania and the facing is from somewhere else. To experience local taste, you don't have modified milk ingredients on the label."

Cheeses made by large food companies with processed milk products are nevertheless being marketed as artisanal to those of us looking for this terroir. The country's largest dairy producer, Saputo, makes a series of cheeses under the name of an apocryphal artisan, Alexis de Portneuf. Their product's marketing material features artsy photographs of an old man on a farm. The various cheeses under this brand have names like La Sauvagine, a soft cheese that won awards in 2008, and evoke the terroir of Quebec. It's easy to be fooled into thinking that these cheeses are really made on a farm by an elderly man.

This is one reason the Société des Fromages du Québec is pushing the provincial government to pass legislation that specifically defines terms

like artisan, *fermier* (farmstead in English) and even terroir, and thus protect the farmers' products. I use the word freely in this book, yet *artisan*
has become practically meaningless as major corporations slap this fuzzy
and warm adjective on a wide range of industrial foods. The Société des
Fromages, however, is starting with the word *fermier*. They want it to
carry a legal definition that means cheese made on the farm from the
milk of that farm's herd. They argue that the farmers have developed this
micro-industry. They have worked to build the food culture in the province, helped to refine the *patrimoine gastronomique*. They are helping to
build this local food economy, and it is they who should reap the benefits.

·   ·   ·

At the Fromagerie La Station, the smell of cedar shingle permeated the
boutique they had only just constructed to help sell cheese to the tourists and Montrealers who visit the Eastern Townships. It's a basic room
with a cash register, a refrigerated case for the cheese, a few tables and a
window onto the *fromagerie* through which people can watch the cheese
being made. A young woman Simon-Pierre had hired to help sell the
cheese offered samples to two customers who had pulled into the driveway. Even though the *fromagerie* had all the hallmarks of a money-making
operation, it was clear that it is the passion of cheese making that drives
Simon-Pierre. "It's not about money. I'm not making eight-month-old
cheese with organic milk to make money," he said with a chuckle. Rather,
he is creating art in the form of food to be enjoyed by many. On their
farm, cheese is culture. Culture that is connected to history and to a way
of living and eating.

CHAPTER EIGHT

CHEFS GO LOCAL

Cooking a New Food Culture in British Columbia

Chef de cuisine Quang Dang commanded his knife masterfully. He stood at the wood-block counter, instrument in one hand, apple from British Columbia positioned by the other. He started slowly, slicing the flesh off the core in three deliberate cuts. Carefully, he divided each piece into two and then lined them up for the final slicing. His hand picked up speed, and paper-thin apple slices blurred by as they slid off the blade. This is step one for the apple, candied walnut and endive salad with a smoked mayo dressing that was on the menu the night I dropped in at Vancouver's C Restaurant. Chef then mixed all the ingredients together in a stainless steel bowl, pinched some salt and, with a flourish of the wrist, tossed it on top. Lucky people will eat chef's salad, prepared by his very own hands—it is unusual in most restaurants for the chef to prepare the salad.

Just a few feet away, the sous-chef (number two in command) and the chef de partie (number three) were busy assembling the entrées. They moved at a steady pace, chins tucked, eyes focused on the frying pan. They reached for squeeze bottles of sauces they needed to turn these dishes into an elaborate show. Then they darted back to the North Arm

Farm's parsnip velouté that was bubbling in a copper saucepan over the gas flame. They plated beef brisket, braised overnight, with caramelized cauliflower and jus made from garlic grown in Agassiz, about a hundred kilometres away. (The menu identifies where the various vegetables have been grown.) The sous-chef took the soup from the stove and pulsed it with a hand blender, splattering his white apron, before pouring the warm liquid into a stainless steel teapot. (The server would then pour it into a bowl placed in front of the patron, drowning some molecular gastronomic blackberry honey pearls she would first place in the bottom.) The chef de partie, wiping his hands on his white apron, made sure the order was fully assembled and then placed a slip of paper on an overhead beam to signal that it was ready. The restaurant manager, a man wearing a black suit and a warm smile despite the chaos of the kitchen, inspected the dish and then shouted, "Service!" A waiter appeared. "We're going to 34. Velouté to 34."

This is a well-honed routine at C, a restaurant known for its sustainable seafood, as well as its locally sourced ingredients of the terrestrial variety. The restaurant is one of a trio of restaurants (the other two are Raincity Grill and Nu) owned by the same investor, all devoted to local food, all occupying dramatic waterfront real estate. Guided by executive chef Robert Clark, it was the first restaurant to partner with the Vancouver Aquarium's Ocean Wise program, a conservation initiative that helps chefs and consumers pick environmentally friendly seafood. It is, arguably, the first sustainable seafood restaurant in the city. But it is pricey. "It's the most expensive restaurant in town," said Clark.

The night I visited C, it was foggy. Really foggy. Big white bats of the stuff somersaulted down the stairs to the restaurant and then in front of the window, obscuring the view of the boats docked in False Creek. Nevertheless, the restaurant was full. Older couples perused the wine menu. Twenty-somethings in parties of four, five and six laughed and clinked their glasses. Well-dressed folks rushed in through the glass doors, leaving their SUVs to be parked by the valet service.

I had come to C because it serves one of the best examples of West Coast regional cuisine in the city. I was visiting Vancouver because it is here where chefs have fostered a local food culture that has seeped out of restaurants and into the kitchens of everyday people. They've helped to make local eating a way of life for the general population.

The 100-mile diet, after all, was conceived of by two Vancouverites, Alisa Smith and J. B. MacKinnon. They popularized the "eat local" culture that only recently came to be but has spread quickly. Twenty-five years ago, you would have been hard pressed to find *any* restaurant in town serving foods sourced in the province. Today, it's practically impossible to achieve culinary stature in Vancouver *without* cooking in the loosely defined style of West Coast regional cuisine—also known as West Coast contemporary, West Coast Canadian and even Pacific North West cuisine. That there isn't an agreed-upon term for this style of cooking is proof of its newness. Whatever you call it, the meaning is the same: local, seasonal and sustainable. Chefs who cook in this way look to the bounty of the province and cook with what's available that day, at that time of the year. It is inspired by Asian cooking styles, specifically Japanese and Chinese, as well as the province's proximity to the Pacific and its rich fish and seafood offerings (though only the sustainably harvested ones).

A West Coast regional menu features creations such as Nu's Salt Spring Island Mussels, double-smoked bacon, leek ribbons, garlic-chipotle cream, and frites. Bishop's restaurant offers grilled Pemberton Meadows beef tenderloin, turnip soufflé, butternut squash purée, watercress and a red wine jus. Blue Water Café and Raw Bar serves lingcod fished off the coast alongside warm celeriac panna cotta, beluga lentils, caramelized salsify and a tarragon mustard jus. Despite their disparate styles and flavours, these varied dishes constitute a cuisine because they share ingredients that are rooted to place, to the geography and climate of British Columbia. "You can close your eyes and know that you are dining in Vancouver," said Jamie Maw, a long-time restaurant critic and food writer who witnessed the evolution of West Coast regional cuisine while he was the food editor of *Vancouver Magazine*. "Local, seasonal, organic, sustainable. Full stop. That's the big thing. In New York there are cuisines from the entire world. But is there an aggregate cuisine? No. Vancouver is a very interesting city in which to watch the culinary DNA weave together. All the cuisines have been woven together to create a common cuisine with influences from elsewhere. You add to that mix local farmers, fishers, ranchers—that's what sets us apart."

Around Vancouver today, in addition to C and its siblings, dozens of restaurants spotlight local cuisine. Maw would argue that the majority of what he deems to be "interesting" restaurants use a preponderance of local ingredients, "sometimes to the point of obsession," he says. While the higher-end restaurants often are devoted to West Coast regional, many other places whose menus have lower prices than C's also cook in this fashion. In fact, the founding principles of the cuisine have even been adopted by establishments that don't necessarily cook in the West Coast regional style, but subscribe to its ethos anyway, such as the casual place Maw likes to visit for a quick bite near Granville Island called Go Fish, where people line up for sustainably harvested fish and chips or fish tacos. Or even celebrity chef Vikram Vij's Rangoli, an Indian eatery with affordable prices and hybrid dishes such as goat meat sourced in British Columbia that is combined in a curry with imported jackfruit, or local organic chicken cooked in an Indian mint, cilantro and yogurt curry. Maw has stood with Vij out in the back alley many times while the chef buys fresh, local, organic ingredients from a truck. By using what is grown around Vancouver in his traditional Indian cuisine, Maw said, Vij is taking West Coast regional to a whole new level. "By using local ingredients, he is creating dishes that do not exist in India. And you get this newly evolved cuisine."

The food these restaurants buy is more local than not, often organic, and grown by some of the smaller-sized farms that are a short drive from the city. This has meant that by cooking with local food, the chefs of Vancouver are supporting a network of farmers and helping to forge a strong, healthy local food system in British Columbia. They are strengthening a new gastronomic culture and creating a culinary identity for the province.

. . .

Anybody I ask about the origins of West Coast regional cuisine says it all started at the Sooke Harbour House, a hotel on the southern tip of Vancouver Island in the small town of Sooke. The House, as people in the know call it, is a boutique hotel run by Sinclair and Frédérique Philip and built overlooking a rocky beach and a small bay. It's a beautiful spot: the rooms are furnished with antiques and filled with West Coast art, and the view of the bay where bald eagles fly, otters play and tides swell is exquisite. From the windows on the southwest side of the hotel, you see few signs of human activity, though the odd tanker ship does move slowly across the horizon. It's in the sunny dining room that gives on to the ocean where, for the last twenty-odd years, the Sooke Harbour House has made its mark on Canada's culinary history by serving local foods prepared with the utmost care. Long before terroir was a word in the average chef's lexicon, the House was discovering and celebrating the terroir of Vancouver Island.

It was a cold January afternoon when I arrived. I was greeted by a sculpture in the parking lot of two killer whales, carved out of wood, jumping out of a wavy sea made of driftwood pieces in which small fish with iridescent blue eyes swim. On the porch in front of the main door is a mosaic of a mermaid in turquoise and pinks. Off to the right, in what appeared to be the winter remains of a formal flower garden, were several rows of mini cold-frame greenhouses, their bubble-like lids propped open to reveal baby lettuces growing in the middle of winter. Immediately I was struck by the whimsicality of the hotel and the way it is rooted in a sense of place—a piece of fertile land at the edge of the sea. It's different from anywhere else I've visited. These were my first clues as to how a new way of looking at food could have been born here.

The sun was starting to set, and a band of red was spreading behind the tall fir trees. Sinclair wanted to show me around outside before it got dark. The hotel was closed for renovations and no guests were present, yet Sinclair wore a formal dark grey suit. He is not too tall, with neatly kept hair and beard and black plastic Versace glasses. He looked more like a fashion designer than a local food guru. When he talked, it was a non-stop stream of information: "This is calendula. This is thyme. That's rosemary." He pointed to plants in various stages of dormancy. "Everything on the property is edible. Everything but the cedar." The plum trees at the back of the house, strung with a tinsel-like airy green lichen, start to provide fruit in late August. The quince trees blossom in the spring and fruit in the fall. The Grand Fir trees, which reach up about ten metres, find their way into many of the foods served here. In the spring, their bright green shoots, which have a strong lemon flavour, are used in savoury dishes or are dried for use in another season. During the rest of the year, the trees' branches infuse a liquid that is used for steaming, in sauces and for sorbets.

"These are edible flowers, day lilies," Sinclair continued. One review of the Sooke Harbour House restaurant that I'd read mentioned day lily anglaise—a crème anglaise made with puréed flowers—served with maple walnut ice cream and rhubarb strudel. "Snowdrops, primula, bay leaf, amaranth, fig, chickweed, kale, fennel." We were at the back of the hotel now, a few metres from the water, and Sinclair paused to look at the view. "I've seen killer whales here, sea lions. And dolphins. Wait." He leaned his head forward, squinting in the direction of a tall, blue-grey bird wading in a tidal pool. "Is that a heron? That doesn't look like the herons we normally get here." The bird picked up a fish in its beak. As it swallowed the fish, Sinclair said, "There are lots of edible foods right here on this beach." Wild seaweed is harvested to eat, as well as seafood for more than just the birds, though the selection has diminished in the last few years, with some species, such as abalone, having been practically fished to extinction. "When we came here, we got 40 percent of our fish live and almost all the shellfish live. Abalone was fresh. It was very easy to get sea urchins and periwinkles. Now we hardly have any fish at all."

The sun had almost set and the temperature was dropping quickly. As we made our way back to the hotel, he pointed to one last piece of this vista that also serves as the restaurant's pantry. On the sloping, grassy shore on the other side of the bay, there were little white specks—sheep. "The lamb we serve here is from that farm."

The ultimate edible landscape.

●

It has always been about food at the Sooke Harbour House. When Frédérique and Sinclair arrived here in 1979 with two young children and opened what amounted to a five-room bed and breakfast and small restaurant, they didn't have a clue that within two decades, they'd make such an impression on the world of fine dining that *Gourmet* magazine would call them the best restaurant in the world for authentic local cuisine. Once you trace their history, it's obvious that their success was no accident. During the early years of their marriage, Sinclair, a Canadian, and, Frédérique, a French national, lived in France, on a farm in a mountainous area to the south of Grenoble that had long-standing food traditions. In the mountains, they watched the locals live as those in the region had lived for hundreds of years, baking their own bread, growing their own vegetables, raising their own livestock and heading off into the mountains to harvest wild mushrooms and medicinal plants—eating and living in synch with the seasons. The years they lived there, they watched and were inspired by that way of life. So when they moved to Canada and settled in Sooke, they brought seeds that they had collected in France and planted bitter greens such as arugula and endive as well as edible flowers in their big garden, just like the French. Sinclair started to forage for mushrooms on Vancouver Island and explore wild foods.

Sinclair knew that this way of life had existed not only in France but in Canada too, as he was raised in a family where people worked for their food. His grandfather on his mother's side grew his own vegetables and fished and hunted in the woods of Ontario, while his dad's father tended to several acres of gardens. The vegetables he grew were then "put up," preserved in a summer kitchen to be used by the family. Sinclair's childhood had been steeped in food knowledge.

"What we did in Sooke that was so radical and revolutionary was what the rest of humanity had done forever," Sinclair laughed. "We grew a lot. We used local fish. We just continued to do what people had always done.

"A number of people have come to us and said that's brilliant. You've invented the Vancouver Island food tradition. When we came here there was an abundance of local foods for Vancouver Island. It didn't occur to us to eat any other way."

From the beginning, Sinclair and Frédérique defined their own cooking style. At first, the restaurant was a small-time affair, with a few tables, but quickly they added to their dining room as word spread about what they were doing. The family lived in the basement and they rented out the rooms upstairs: they needed money to pay the mortgage. But by the mid-1980s, they were attracting substantial praise. The restaurant was written up in the *Globe and Mail* and *Gourmet*. They expanded their dedication to good food even further by leasing a nearby farm, where they raised livestock as well as grew some vegetables for the restaurant. They met wildcrafters, or foragers, who sold them mushrooms collected in the woods, seaweeds harvested from the oceans. And they learned about the way the local First Nations people used to cook from Nancy Turner, an ethnobotanist who has written at length about the food history of the people who first inhabited the area. It was she who told them about using Grand Fir for flavour and taught them to use cedar boxes, filled with stones heated in a fire, to boil a broth and steam seafood, a dish you can order today in the restaurant.

During this period, a number of chefs passed through the kitchen, including Michael Stadtländer, before he became famous for embracing the ethos of local cooking. The chefs created their own recipes and added to the distinct cooking style. There is the opportunity to experiment in the kitchen, since the chef de cuisine is given flexibility. Because they change the menu daily, depending on what the fishers or the wildcrafters have brought in, there is a lot of room for experimentation; the variety is so great that some dishes are only ever made once. Although Sinclair himself never cooked, he has become the grandfather of West Coast regional cuisine. It was his and Frédérique's vision that defined what Sooke Harbour House would be. Sinclair, with the help of people like Dr. Turner and the various chefs who passed through the place, encouraged the public to reconsider how they saw food. They broadened the definition of *edible* and inspired two generations of chefs to continue exploring just what "local, seasonal and sustainable" means on the restaurant table.

"A lot of Vancouver chefs worked at Sooke Harbour House," said Jamie Maw of Sinclair's influence on the Vancouver scene. "They brought back that ethos of cooking locally and sustainably. His influence was massive."

. . .

"Local, seasonal and sustainable" sounds delicious, but to be able to support an entire restaurant industry that wants to cook in this way, you need infrastructure. The role chefs play in the local food system in Canada goes beyond defining a new cuisine. The men and women who run these dozens and dozens of restaurant kitchens have been instrumental in building a localized foodshed in British Columbia. They have helped to shape new distribution networks and provided farmers with a market for their produce, making growing for local buyers a viable livelihood. When Robert Clark started at C in 1997, the notion of cooking with local ingredients had only recently become mainstream. At that time, despite the success of the Sooke Harbour House, "we as Canadians were very insecure," he remembered. "If we wanted to present wines, we'd present French wines.

We were part of a world food culture and we'd use blueberries from Chile. Cuisine was geared to bringing in stuff from offshore." Clark had arrived in British Columbia from Toronto, where he had worked with legendary chef Jamie Kennedy, who has long been a devotee of local foods, and learned the importance of sourcing his ingredients from a specific region. By the time he got to C, Clark was ready to take on the job of defining the kind of food they would serve by finding local suppliers for the seafood, meat and vegetables on their menu. The owner of C and its sibling restaurants wanted his businesses to be the first to define West Coast regional cuisine.

In the 1990s, it was the local organic farmers who were pushing chefs to move in this new direction. They would drive up to the kitchen doors of Vancouver restaurants, their trucks laden with produce you couldn't have bought anywhere else at the time, like mesclun greens (this was before there were large plastic boxes of mesclun at the grocery store selling for five bucks), fresh herbs and heirloom tomatoes. "It was an exciting thing for us because the truck would pull up and you'd buy baby fennel. Chefs want variety. We always want to be serving what the guy down the street can't get. It was expensive, but the economics made sense because you were buying stuff you couldn't get anywhere else." The farmers selling the organic vegetables would educate the chefs, introducing them to all sorts of different vegetable treats, and the chefs in turn would put them on their menus and educate the public, who would then want to make in their own kitchens what they were eating in restaurants. (This is how these organic mesclun greens became as common as Caesar salad with bacon bits.)

C wasn't the only restaurant in town on the local-and-sustainable path. Not too far away, in the trendy neighbourhood of Kitsilano, chef John Bishop had been cooking local food in his eponymously named restaurant, Bishop's, for a decade. Through the mid-1980s and into the 1990s, Bishop's collaborated with local farmers like Naty and Gary King of Hazelmere Organic Farm, in Surrey, to create menus that were reflective of what was being grown around the city; the restaurant's menu has featured dishes such as Hazelmere Farm celeriac soup.

These days in Vancouver's restaurants, the chefs don't wait for farmers to arrive at the back door. Restaurants like C and Bishop's have a network of farmers they work with, year after year. The collaboration can be so close that in the winter, some chefs will even sit down with the farmers and go through seed catalogues, choosing what vegetables they would like to cook with the coming summer. At C, Clark still makes sure he gets to know the people who supply his food. He goes fishing with the salmon fishers; he visits the farms when he starts to buy from someone new. And he won't hesitate to try a farmer's new products. For example, the man from whom they purchase their salmon farms the fish sustainably, in a closed-pen environment. He started to raise crayfish, which are now served at C, and diverts the waste water from the salmon through hydroponic channels in which he grows wasabi and watercress, also now used at the restaurant. The night I visited C, Chef Quang offered me a beet salad made from pickled and puréed beets they preserved in summer, and the plate was garnished with a dab of this very watercress purée.

Selling to restaurants is good for farmers too. They are able to plant their crops in the spring knowing they have a guaranteed buyer for what they grow. Plus, chefs are prepared to pay for quality; they will give the farmers more than a wholesaler ever would. Time and time again, across the country, the farmers and chefs I interviewed while writing this book told me that chefs pay the most for raw ingredients. The people whose artistic medium is carrots and lamb and scallops and beets know that cheap food is generally not good food. To make a spectacular meal, you need spectacular ingredients. This allows farmers to make a decent wage. In addition, selling to restaurants offers a critical mass. "If you wanted three hundred people to eat sustainable tonight, it takes a lot of effort to convince them to buy it and cook it at home," said Clark. "But all you have to do is convince one chef, and everyone who comes in to that restaurant will eat it. I believe it's very important that every inch of farmland today should be farmland one hundred years from now. The only way to stop farmers from selling to developers is to be able to create a sustainable system that allows a couple to raise a family. That is my goal."

Back in Sooke, it's a similar story. You don't become one of the most famous restaurants in Canada without serving the best foods, made with the best ingredients. They offer incredible dishes, like yellow-split-pea-encrusted lingcod with carrot and mint emulsion. They serve grilled albacore tuna with a carrot-calendula cream, crispy seaweed and smoked salmon barley roll, fiddlehead morels and a yellow onion–pumpkin seed dressing. Or Cackleberry Farm rabbit marinated in juniper and red wine, served with apricot, chili and mint sauces, maple glazed carrots, greens and a house-cured ham frittata. A four-course meal easily costs under a hundred dollars a person. Even the room-service menu is a delectable read: Berkshire cured pork shoulder and raclette-style cheese sandwich with red onion relish. Or how about crispy Fanny Bay oysters on root vegetable–cilantro slaw.

The Harbour House grows some of the more uncommon vegetables they use in their dishes on their nearby farm to supplement the edible plants on the grounds. They also rely on a few chosen farmers for supplies. Two of those farmers are Mary Alice Johnson and Marika Nagasaka of ALM Organic Farm, which is a short, winding drive away from the hotel. Theirs is a small, mixed organic farm amid the old cedar forest that still covers much of Vancouver Island. Mary Alice, who is nearing retirement, and twenty-nine-year-old Marika raise pigs and chickens and grow a wide variety of vegetables they sell to the hotel. Marika and the chef at the House have worked closely over the years. She loves to drive her produce in to Sooke every Wednesday. The chef gives her cookies and they find time to talk. "It's like we give them the colours of the palette they use," she said of their relationship. "They get so excited and they really feed my creative side. They help me value what we do. I love it when they explain to me what they are going to do with it. 'Oh, those turnips, here's what I did with them.'"

·　·　·

The West Coast might be a hot spot of regional cuisine in Canada, but chefs across the country are working to develop their own styles too. At Calgary's River Café, chef Scott Pohorelic crafts such delicacies as handmade perogies filled with native grass-fed bison. He braises wild boar, elk and deer and makes a popular wild rice pudding. In Manitoba, chefs also are seeking out farms that don't service the export agriculture economy and instead grow vegetables and raise livestock. Just outside Montreal, chef Martin Picard of the restaurant Au Pied de Cochon also runs a sugar shack where he serves foods inspired by local tradition and involving plenty of maple syrup. He is just one of the many Québécois chefs who are inspired by the bounty of the province. In the Maritimes, chefs such as Chris Aerni at the Rossmount Inn in St. Andrews by-the-Sea serve local delicacies like weir-caught herring—"They are so small and magnificent," he said of the fish that are caught in the traditional traps. Also on offer is a full range of summer fruits and vegetables and what Chris calls a "brown and yellow menu" in the winter, composed of legumes and root vegetables from the region.

In Ontario, it was über-chefs Jamie Kennedy and Michael Stadtländer who are often credited with launching the local-food movement on Toronto's fine-dining scene in the 1980s and went on to popularize the idea of cooking locally grown produce as a way of developing the taste of a region. Kennedy, who grew up in the Toronto suburb of Don Mills, met Stadtländer, a German national, when they were both cooking in Switzerland. When Kennedy received an offer to become the chef de cuisine at Toronto's renowned Scaramouche at the stunningly young age of twenty-three, he accepted the job on the condition that he could bring

Stadtländer. For the next few years, the two chefs devoted themselves to the Michelin three-star model. As at any other fine-dining establishment in the country, they believed that to cook fabulous food, you had to use ingredients from a fabulous place, and that place was France. What they did at Scaramouche was the antithesis of the local cuisine the two men are known for today. To obtain items such as foie gras or the proper fish for bouillabaisse, they had an agent who took their shopping list to Paris's Rungis Market, one of the largest wholesale food markets in the world. These most-French-of-French delicacies were then loaded onto a plane and flown to Scaramouche's kitchen in Toronto.

But, slowly, they lost interest in this way of cooking. "It lost its allure," said Kennedy. He started to pay attention to what Ontario had to offer. "All through my childhood and into my cooking years, I always knew there was excellent stuff out there. I'd drive up north and eat blueberries or peaches. They were amazing. But I never had that in the restaurant. Michael and I were so tired with the status quo that we got from our suppliers." When they turned to local ingredients and realized that they could cook with them too, "it was a great awakening and a shift. We didn't need to bring things from away."

Kennedy decided to open his own restaurant, The Palmerston, where he went on to develop his new style of cooking. Around the same time, he and Statdländer decided they wanted to help other chefs access the foods that Canada, not France, had to offer. They started a non-profit they called Knives and Forks, which promoted the benefits of local agriculture. And they launched a market where their colleagues could buy the freshest of ingredients directly from farmers, introducing their peers to the benefits of working with Ontario's ingredients. It was also Knives and Forks that came up with the idea of the Feast of Fields, a harvesttime feast hosted by chefs and farmers that is open to the public and has become a phenomenon, with feasts organized annually in Ontario and British Columbia. Although the organization itself didn't last for long, it helped the spirit of local food take hold in Toronto. Slowly, more and more chefs started to cook with foods from the immediate area. Decades after it began, the momentum is picking up again. "The younger generation of chefs emerging now is embracing this ideology in a way that is unprecedented," said Kennedy. "It's wide and deep. I think it has a lot to do with the city maturing culturally. Food-culture wise. Gastronomically. We're comfortable in our own skin."

. . .

In Saskatoon, a similar keeper of local food knowledge is a place called Calories Restaurant, a cozy bistro with a dessert counter at the front and a chalkboard high on the wall on which the lunch menu is written daily. Dinner is more formal, but all meals feature ingredients from Saskatchewan. Rémi Cousyn is the chef here. He's a charming man, whose dark, wide-set eyes come to life when he talks about local foods and the important role chefs have in preserving a way of cooking, in preserving a culture. Cousyn grew up in France, near Nice, where he started to cook at the age of sixteen. It was his wife, Janis, a Canadian dancer who was working in Europe, who brought him to Canada and to her hometown, Saskatoon. They came to Calories in 1995 as business partners, and Rémi started to cook in his trademark fashion, which wasn't easy. "Getting stuff here is really difficult," he said. "Being in the middle of nowhere and needing to get stuff in . . ." His voice trailed off and he shook his head. "This was thirteen years ago! It still scares people away today." In a handful of restaurants in the city, chefs have more recently turned to the province's small farmers to source their foods, but the vast majority of ingredients are shipped into the province.

Cousyn takes his commitment to local food very seriously, ensuring that the restaurant purchases absolutely everything they can from nearby, that every dish they serve is prepared from scratch. To preserve the harvest, they make jams and fruit preserves and pickles out of asparagus, cucumbers, beets and more. They butcher lamb and pork themselves, using all the meat from snout to tail. When they cook poultry, they don't waste any part of the quail, duck or chicken. They make their own corned beef, salt pork, smoked fish and foie gras. His next experiment will be to make cheese. When they make soup, they start at the beginning by boiling bones for stock. Their desserts are homemade, as is their hollandaise sauce. They sweeten their drinks with Saskatchewan honey and they use organic grains grown nearby for their bread. They even make ketchup—Cousyn tells the farmers to throw the bruised tomatoes they can't sell fresh into the freezer and he'll buy them. "I push the envelope as much as I can so the farmers can ramp up production."

The difference between Cousyn's kitchen and the vast majority of restaurants in Canada is very simple. Casual dining chains, the kind of restaurants you find in malls and plazas where you'll spend upwards of $15 on a pasta dish or a grilled chicken Caesar, as well as independent restaurants, pubs, hotels and even catering companies, often don't make the food they serve. Cousyn himself cooks, whereas most places order processed foods from a catalogue—from hollandaise sauce to frozen butter chicken to instant potatoes to lemon meringue pie. In these popular restaurants, the cooks open a package, reheat the prepared food and present it to look as if some chef concocted a lovely dish for you. At Calories, they are actually *cooking*.

Just as the home cook is disappearing, so too is the cook in your average family restaurant or pub. Most menus feature boil-in-a-bag soups, frozen meat and seafood entrées and prefab sauces procured from one of the major restaurant suppliers, such as Kraft, Sisco and E.D. Smith. Even the sandwich at your local bistro may not have been made in-house. AFC Food Group, a Toronto-based company whose pre-made "freeze and thaw" pasta products, sandwiches and baked goods are sold to restaurants, cafés and retail chains under the Amore Foods brand, sells handmade-style prefabricated sandwiches. "Our unique approach to food production allows us to take advantage of cost efficiencies while providing café quality products with a handmade touch," reads the promotional material on their website. The sandwiches are packaged with what is called a micro-wave crisper unit so that after they are heated, the bread will taste "just like a fresh made sandwich from your local café or deli."

Even if they are cooking from scratch, restaurants depend on imports to keep Caesar salad or tomatoes and bocconcini or spicy fried eggplant on the menu every single day of the year. The vast majority of the restaurant industry is embedded in the global food chain. Much of the food in motion at this very second—in ship containers, packed into the cargo hold of airplanes or loaded onto tractor-trailers—is destined for restaurants. And it's not only the big chains. Hotel restaurants, the fanciest of fine-dining establishments, right down to the mom-and-pop counter in the food court, all are serving farmed shrimp from Thailand and air-freighted Chilean raspberries. In 2005, in Canada there were 63,000 food-service establishments, and they sold approximately $45 billion worth of food. These figures demonstrate the importance of involving the restaurant industry in future change.

In order to build a sustainable food system in Canada, the restaurant industry needs to be a leader. If all that purchasing power were directed at supporting local farms, a regional food system would likely thrive. For this to happen, we need new distribution channels, replacing long-distance supply chains with regional ones. And restaurants, as well as their patrons, must become more flexible. In any restaurant that cooks with the seasons, menus change according to what's available. There might not be local asparagus in February, but there would be root vegetable slaw with a creamy dressing—and eaters would have to learn to wait until the right season for that dish they like best. The food-preparation skills that Rémi Cousyn is preserving in Saskatoon would have to be adopted by chefs across the country.

The hurdle, of course, is cost. Restaurants serve prepared food because it's ultimately cheaper. Because labour costs are high in North America, to increase their profits, many restaurants lower their costs by cutting what they spend on food. When you don't have to pay someone to make the lasagna or the hollandaise, what you save boosts your profit margins. To process so much food from its raw form into a pickle or a piece of charcuterie or a loaf of bread, Cousyn has a staff of forty-five—for a restaurant that seats fifty-five. Most of his costs are in payroll. "It takes one hour and a half to break down a lamb and wrap it up. But if you open a package of rack of lamb, pre-seasoned, from one of these catalogues, put it in the oven, it's on the plate in twelve minutes. People will pay $36 for that rack of lamb, and the real cost of that labour is peanuts."

Cousyn overcomes this problem by working with apprentice chefs and teaching them how to do things the old-fashioned way, from scratch. In this way, he is educating a new generation of chefs. Not only do they gain a solid appreciation of local foods but Cousyn arms the apprentices with the knowledge of how to turn food in its raw form into a spectacular meal. And he is unabashedly political about it. Cousyn believes that the changes he and others make in the restaurant community have a real impact on the rest of society. By teaching people by example how to eat local foods, he believes he can shape how they eat every day at home. "The knowledge of being able to cook that local food is to have the right to cook it however you want. Not having it pre-fried, pre-seasoned, pre-cooked. It's about having the control to eat what you want," he said. "Once the big food companies have killed the local knowledge, we will have lost everything."

·

When I visited Sooke, I got a clear picture of just how far the restaurant industry is from Cousyn's ideal. It was January, and the town's restaurants that were devoted to local foods were closed for a winter break. Sinclair and I headed out to eat at a trendy Thai place, with lime green walls and tables full of locals eating tom yum. When he asked where the shrimp in the curry came from, the waitress told us it had been ordered from a food-service catalogue, which meant it had been farmed somewhere far away (despite the ready availability of local, sustainable shrimp caught nearby). We chose chicken. For real change to take place, the food courts where so many of us buy lunch, the family restaurants where we go with our kids, all these places will need to embrace the idea of buying from the surrounding region.

It's easy to think that change of such magnitude is impossible, or at least unlikely. Yet the North American restaurant industry has proven itself able to respond to consumer demand in the past. McDonald's eliminated their super-size menu in response to market pressures, and in New York City, when a new law required chains to show the number of calories in their products right on the menu, restaurants amended their recipes. A 1,187-calorie blueberry-pomegranate smoothie at one chain quickly turned into a 550-calorie drink.

Marion Nestle, a professor in the Department of Nutrition, Food Studies and Public Health at New York University, has written extensively about the food industry. She believes that a restaurant will respond to public pressure. "The restaurant's job is to sell food," she told me. "So the question is, can they incorporate ideals and ideology and still sell food? The answer is yes. This could start small. If every restaurant in Toronto decided it wanted to source some of its ingredients fresh, that would have an incredible impact on the local farms. You want to start by creating a small demand, and that will encourage a larger demand."

Already this is starting to happen.

. . .

During the average Friday lunch-hour rush, which starts at noon and ends around one, the line cooks at the Il Fornello restaurant on King Street West in Toronto will make 120 pizzas. That works out to one thin-crust, handmade, wood-fired pizza every thirty seconds. The pizzas are prepared in an area that gives onto the 180-seat restaurant so customers can watch the line cooks slide pies into the ovens, see the flames and the burning embers cooking the dough. As I watched one fall noon hour, four men moved steadily but speedily, smoothing tomato sauce onto rounds of dough, sprinkling them with mushrooms, cheese and sausages or any of the toppings in the thirty stainless steel containers, transferring them to the oven, then sliding them onto plates and out onto a large counter, where they are paired with a salad and whisked away by a waiter.

Il Fornello is a Toronto-area Italian chain that is a big step up from fast food, and the meals served here are better in quality than you would find in similarly priced large chain restaurants. Il Fornello is also a chain, with nine locations across the Greater Toronto Area serving the same prosciutto pizza and pasta Bolognese at every location. Ian Sorbie, the chain's owner, founded the restaurant in the late 1980s. In 2007, he had his own local-food epiphany, and realized that the choices we make when we eat (or, in his case, serve) have a direct impact on the world.

Sorbie owns a hobby farm in Prince Edward County in Eastern Ontario, where small vineyards, family farmers and artisanal food producers have sparked a local-food revival. Not far from his place are at least half a dozen farm-gate stands where anyone can buy organic veggies and fresh eggs laid by hens that eat grass and insects. One day, he was standing in his field, listening to the hum of the tractor as the neighbouring farmer baled his hay. He could also hear cows mooing, ready to be milked, even a rooster crowing, and he was almost in tears. "My God, I thought. We've forgotten the hard work these farmers do." He realized that in his role as restaurateur, he could support these farmers, and so he came up with a new buying protocol for the Il Fornello chain.

Sorbie went back to Toronto and hired an executive chef, Owen Steinberg, who tracked down a number of local farmers who could supply the restaurant with everything from the butternut squash for their soup to arugula for their salad and their own canned tomato sauce, made in Canada's tomato capital, Leamington, Ontario. He sent the restaurant's buyer to the Ontario Food Terminal every morning to purchase the vegetables they needed, with strict instructions to buy local first and imported second, even if the price was higher. The restaurant went as far as to offer its own private-label spring water sourced nearby, as an ecological alternative to the San Pellegrino mineral water that is shipped from Italy.

The menu did well. The Ontario heirloom tomato pizza, with green-and-yellow zebra and ruby-coloured tomatoes, was particularly delicious because it showcased local tomatoes at their prime. But then the recession hit towards the end of 2008, and people stopped eating out as much. Sorbie, still idealistic but now fiscally nervous, pulled back from his local menu in January 2009. They dropped the prices in the restaurant, but that meant they could no longer afford the cost of local produce across the board. Il Fornello wasn't the only restaurant to feel the pinch. A few months later, Jamie Kennedy announced that he would be selling one of his establishments because business was down.

These two cases raise the question of how we can take the success of West Coast regional cuisine and marry it to the way the majority of us eat in Canada. How can we sustain this healthy relationship between chefs and farmers and help it to withstand both faddism and recession? According to Jamie Kennedy, a cultural shift is necessary. People from all walks of life must care about food and want to eat from their own region. He calls this "gastronomy of place"—a concept not unlike *patrimoine gastronomique*—and defines it as a cuisine rooted in geography. Only when this concept seizes the collective imagination will a local food system truly take hold.

. . .

It was dark when I arrived at the Smoken Bones Cookshack in Langford, a suburb of Victoria. I took a wrong turn and ended up driving first through a commercial area lined with big-box American stores and then into a typical North American subdivision of single-family houses and two-car garages. The place was deserted. It felt like a Sunday night. Finally, after a few U-turns, I found my way to the Cookshack. It must have been where everyone in Langford was eating that night, because there was only one spot left in the parking lot. Inside was like a bar during the Stanley Cup finals. It was noisy. Half a dozen TVs were positioned around the room, and all the tables were packed with families, couples and older folks. They were all tucking into plates piled high with ribs.

The Cookshack's specialty is large portions of Southern-style food that you can eat with your hands. There are no pretensions about the place. The optional cutlery is found in a bucket on each table, the booths are vinyl, and the food is simple and plenty. When my order arrived, it looked like something out of the Flintstones. A heap of bones dominated my plate, with a pile of greens and root vegetables drenched in butter on the side. I picked up a rib and took a bite. It was absolutely delicious. The meat was moist, flaking off the bone, and the flavour was deep and smoky—like a smouldering fire, not the cloying taste of smoke-in-a-bottle you can buy at the store. The collard greens were smooth and almost sweet. The meal was 100 percent local and unlike anything I'd ever eaten in a restaurant devoted to local food.

That's the point, said Ken Hueston, chef and owner of the Cookshack—he's the Ken in Smo*ken* Bones. Ken is committed to cooking with locally grown ingredients in a way that is accessible to everyone. "My theory about this restaurant is that it should be vernacular," he said. "Most people will do a beet tartar with a crostini and a little doodalee-do. Nuh-uh. I believe in the shabby-chic thing." Pointing to the vinyl tablecloths and the televisions as proof, he said he believes that his restaurant epitomizes a new local-food order in which food grown or raised nearby is the building block of all varieties of cuisines. And on Vancouver Island, chefs like Ken have led the way by enticing the public to eat regionally.

The Island Chefs' Collaborative was founded in 1999 by a group of chefs who wanted to guarantee access to the ingredients they used in their kitchens—Ken is a past president. The chefs wanted to work with farmers so they would grow the foods the restaurants desired while the farmers' businesses could not only survive but thrive. The larger ideal behind the collaborative was to help foster an alternative food system on the Island that could feed the general public.

Chefs aren't necessarily known for their political action, but these men and women were motivated to found such a political organization because they were losing their local suppliers. Each year, a beloved grower of asparagus or onions or spinach would close their farm. "All these terrible things were happening to farmers," remembered David Mincey, owner and chef at Camille's Restaurant in Victoria and one of the group's founders. "Their land was going to be turned into subdivisions. Together as an organization with a name and a mission we might be able to have an effect on this."

Just like in the rest of Canada, farming on the Island is fraught. The average age of farmers is about fifty-five, and most plan to retire within the next decade. On the whole, the younger generation isn't interested in agriculture, and those who are have a hard time acquiring land. Even though farmland is protected by British Columbia's Agricultural Land Reserve, its speculative value—its potential value if it were turned into building lots—has driven up prices, making it hard for young people to buy land. Then there are problems that are particular to the Island. Local poultry farmers hold only enough quota to raise 20 percent of the chickens that are consumed here (poultry farming works on a supply management system, which means a local poultry board decides how many birds each farmer can raise), leaving grocery stores no choice but to primarily source elsewhere. Changes to the provincial abattoir legislation are being blamed for driving small abattoirs out of business and leaving farmers with fewer and fewer places to process their meat. When farming is in trouble, so are the chefs. They understand that the food they serve is tied directly to the fate of the farm.

Tom Henry, a farmer and author of a book about agriculture on the Island, understands this relationship well. Henry is also the editor of the magazine *Small Farm Canada,* which he founded. He and his wife, Violaine Mitchell, run a small mixed farm, not unlike others in the area, where he raises sheep and hogs and grows forty acres of grains. He has made a name for himself on the Island as a leader in sustainable agriculture, not only because of how he farms but also because of the way he thinks and talks about farming and society.

I felt like I'd arrived in utopia when I stepped onto the land at his farm, in the town of Metchosin; it is one of the most beautiful farms I've ever visited. A herd of sheep grazed on the grassy pasture at the top of a thirty-metre-high bluff overlooking the Juan de Fuca Strait. Under towering pine trees, the white-coated sheep munched on the winter grasses. The January sun sparkled on the blue of the water below. Over in the distance, beyond the curving shoreline of beach and forest, was the shade of an outline of the city of Victoria.

After a brief chat in the living room, Henry and I headed off for a walk about the property, and we continued to discuss the issues he's thought a lot about. He wore a wide-brimmed hat and jeans and took enormous strides that seemed to get longer with each passionate sentence. What makes this place different from other parts of Canada, he said, is that agriculture on Vancouver Island bottomed out about forty years ago, several decades before the same thing happened in the rest of the country. In other parts of Canada, the 1960s were a boom time for farmers who wanted to follow the government's advice and "modernize." These farmers increased the size of their farms and bought more machinery with the help of government programs and bank loans. However, Vancouver Island's farmers did not follow suit. They simply didn't have the same opportunity to grow—there's a finite amount of farmland on the Island,

and it wasn't suited to modern, industrial agriculture. "The rest of Canada got big. We couldn't get big because there isn't the farmland. You can't have a nine-thousand-acre farm here. So we got out." That's how the Island went from supplying 85 percent of its own food in the sixties to less than 10 percent today.

Once agriculture started to disappear, people quickly forgot that farming had been the economic backbone and pride of the place. "If you look through the newspaper records of the 1920s, at any of the small towns of Vancouver Island," said Henry, "you'll see agriculture, not forestry, was prime. The Cowichan Valley was famous for its poultry, their hatchery industry. It was called the egg basket of Canada. The Gulf Islands were known for their greenhouses. And some of the best dairy cattle in the Commonwealth was here." But when the sector started to shrink, it was forestry that took over as the economic focus, and people no longer remembered what used to be there.

Strangely, though, the early collapse of the farming sector could end up being its benefit, argues Henry. The fact that farming practically disappeared has made it easier for people to reimagine what it means to farm on Vancouver Island today. "It was because this happened earlier on Vancouver Island than elsewhere—that we lost our connection to agriculture. That allowed people to see new options. You have to have a collapse before you rebuild." This is one reason small farms practising sustainable methods are making a comeback on the Island. Many of these farms are organic, or at least avoid using chemical fertilizers and pesticides even if they don't have official certification. "The rebuilding is taking the form of vineyards, herbs, tree fruit, nuts. We're seeing people tapping trees for syrup. There are people making wine from alder," said Henry. Who better to champion these innovative food products but the local chefs?

The Island Chefs' Collaborative has grown since its inception; today it has dozens of members. They run a farmers' market in Victoria's Bastion Square. They organize events to introduce farmers to the public and oversee a canning program for which chefs make preserves from local produce to sell. Their products are being met with enthusiasm. And since chefs are trendsetters in cuisine, they've been instrumental in popularizing the local-food ethos. Demand for local food is now so great that there are simply not enough farmers growing what consumers want to buy. Sandra Mark, a founder of the Heritage Foodservice Co-op, an organization that is working to build infrastructure to support a regional foodshed here, said this gap in the supply is often called the Island Diet Dilemma.

The chefs also put their money behind the cause. They established an annual grant for farmers on the Island. Each year the money they've raised goes to help with projects like new irrigation systems on small farms, fence building, and other infrastructural improvements such as greenhouses for winter growing. They want to make sure the farms that grow their food stay healthy, ensuring they'll have access to great ingredients all the time. Today on the Island, chefs can fill an entire menu with local foods right through the winter. "It's made farmers viable who wouldn't have been before," said David Mincey. "The best part of it is that you can see the impact of it on people. People are asking for recipes. They are trying vegetables they never would have in the past. There has been a cultural shift."

A cultural shift, a gastronomy of place. The chefs of Vancouver Island have helped to give rise to that elusive but important factor that allows a local food economy to thrive in today's world. Cultural change is one of the most important pieces in the puzzle of local food for Canada.

GROWING UTOPIA

This local-food journey of mine started with a cookie and finishes with one too. At the end of my travels westbound across the country to visit the many people who are building a new and sustainable food system in Canada, I stopped at the Wild Fire Bakery in Victoria, where they use local, organic ingredients and often heritage grains like Red Fife wheat to make their cookies, breads and muffins from scratch. The bakery is not far from the tourist strip downtown, in a one-storey brick building covered with street art. One of the murals outside depicts a group of sharks dressed in business suits sitting around a table with stacks of money and the words "Power Corrupts" written above. It was early in the morning when I arrived, but the place was busy. Customers lined up for their morning fare while a number of young people bustled about behind the counter, pulling loaves and muffins from the ovens.

Even though I had just eaten my breakfast, I bought a cookie. I couldn't resist the shortbread made with Red Fife—grown by Tom Henry, whose farm I'd visited in Metchosin and who is one of the bakery's suppliers. The cookies were a deep golden brown, with red flecks from the bran of the wheat. But it wasn't until later, long after I'd eaten the cookie, that I realized its significance. If the pink-iced cookie that my daughter received in her loot bag years ago summed up all that was wrong with the industrial food system, then this cookie represented what is *right* about the new local food system that we are building in Canada today. This cookie was made with grains grown by a farmer who is practising sustainable agriculture. It was made in a bakery, by people who are keeping alive the culture of making shortbread, the culture of creating food from scratch. And it was delicious. The Red Fife gave the cookie a nutty flavour that paired beautifully with the mellow taste of butter.

This shortbread cookie was a symbol of change that prompted me to reflect on what I'd learned about local food in Canada and tally up what is required for a sustainable system to thrive here. I began my list.

On the farm, we need to move towards a holistic understanding of agriculture that takes its cues from nature, supports biodiversity and relies less and less on fossil fuels. Farmers must make a living wage and be respected for their work, something achieved by rehumanizing the food chain and connecting farmers with consumers through farmers' markets and community-supported agriculture while at the same time developing new supply chains for institutions such as universities and hospitals. When devising our new food system, we need not dwell on the past and replicate subsistence agriculture. Instead, we can push forward to fashion something new and innovative, using our technology and our imagination to design energy-efficient greenhouses and other novel ways of producing food.

In the city, we need to grow some of what we eat and figure out how to incorporate food production into the metropolis. By connecting with the food chain, and eating well, we will be more likely to experience a cultural shift and watch a gastronomy of place take hold.

A 2009 report put out by the International Assessment of Agricultural Knowledge, Science, and Technology for Development, a United

Nations-led panel that examined the current state of global agriculture and food production, identified small-scale, sustainable agriculture that combines technical know-how with traditional knowledge as the preferable model for agriculture and food production on this planet. When the panel of four hundred of the world's experts convened to study the state of agriculture, their goal was to figure out how best to support an economically and environmentally sustainable food system that provides enough calories for a growing world population. The intent was to be descriptive rather than proscriptive, in the hope that governments would heed the findings and shape their policies accordingly. At the base of the panel's conclusions is a belief that science and technology should be married with traditional knowledge in a new approach to agriculture.

.

I had seen first-hand evidence of versions of such a system taking hold across Canada. However, up until the very end of my travels, I had not yet explored the importance of traditional knowledge, which in the Canadian context includes the food knowledge of the people who lived and ate on this piece of land long before Europeans arrived here. So the final stop on my local-food journey was a visit to an ecological restoration project at the Tsawout First Nation reserve in Saanich, a suburb of Victoria. There, people are trying to reclaim the food traditions of their ancestors that have been almost erased by colonialism and the cultural devastation of residential schools. Similar efforts are taking place across Vancouver Island, but it is a challenge. The people who are trying to preserve what's left of the old ways have never tasted some of the plants they are learning about and would have a hard time finding them in the wild if they were to look. Even their parents and sometimes their grandparents wouldn't have eaten the old foods. By looking back, however, they believe we might be able to envision something new for the future.

I met Earl Claxton Jr. and John-Bradley William, known as JB, at the band office. Earl is an unassuming man of almost sixty, who wore plaid flannel pants, a fleece jacket and a traditional peaked Kazak felted hat he picked up at a Slow Food conference he attended in Italy a few years before. With the conical hat and the casual attire, Earl didn't appear to be the powerhouse he is. He fought for years to preserve First Nations fisheries on the Island and has been recognized internationally for his work. He and JB, who is three decades his junior, are working on several ecological restoration projects. Together, they are trying to revive the indigenous plants that would have fed their ancestors not that long ago.

The two men are enamoured with ecology, plants and the way humans can, if they want, live in harmony with nature while harvesting what they need to live. Their main project is restoring the Cordova Spit, which extends from the reserve into the Saanich Bay. They are transforming it from a party spot where people used to drive their cars on the sand, destroying the native flora, into an ecologically protected zone that resembles the landscape Earl remembers from his childhood when his grandmother used to bring him down to pick medicinal herbs like *q'ǝxmín* —it sounds like "gucmean" in English—that was used to treat tuberculosis, and foods like wild celery. While I have always thought of local as something that is grown here as opposed to there, Earl and JB see local as being synonymous with indigenous.

The spit is a strip of sandy soil a few hundred metres long. It's windblown, with a few shrubs and thin grasses in an area that has been fenced off as part of the restoration project. Despite their hard work, the land appeared to be wounded. It was only about five years ago that the water was polluted with fecal coliform from agricultural runoff and from when people used to dump their garbage there. It has improved a lot since then, but the day I visited, there were still tire marks in the earth and a sparseness of flora that gave the impression that the men had a long way to go. But Earl and JB were optimistic. They pointed out all the different edible plants we passed. Every step they took was filled with best intentions.

They bent to collect garbage. Earl stopped to pick a gumweed seed head from the previous summer, now dry and bulging. He pressed it between his fingers to spread the genetic material and hopefully grow some more plants. JB narrated the whole time, pointing out everything edible.

"This is silverweed," he said. You can eat the rhizome roots, the taproot and the leaves. "It's dark green on top," he said, fingering the leaf, "but underneath it looks silver. You steam it. I've tried the leaves. It tastes really bitter." We moved on. "Sourgrass tastes like lemon. This is sea rocket. You can only find it in spring. You use it as a spice to flavour food. The seed head has some heat. It tastes like pepper."

That coming summer, JB was planning to eat camas for the first time. Camas is a lily, and JB's ancestors would have eaten the bulbs regularly. On Vancouver Island, he told me, when the white man arrived—the *hunitum* in their language, meaning "person who appeared"; in another language spoken at the time, the word for white man meant "person we must feed"—his ancestors had a food system that relied on wild foods. While they weren't exactly farmers as we would define the role today, they did cultivate the wild foods they liked to eat, such as Pacific crab apple and camas lilies. When the first Europeans came over what is now called Mount Newton, a mountain not too far from Victoria's airport, and looked down into the Tsawout territory and saw an expanse of blue in the valley below, they thought they were seeing a lake. But what these men were looking at was actually a camas lily meadow, fields and fields of a beautiful blue flower with an edible bulb.

Camas was eaten as a potato-like staple by the Coast Salish peoples on southern Vancouver Island, and also in other areas of British Columbia. It was called the queen root. JB's ancestors would have tended to camas patches, loamy prairie they cleared and burned regularly to encourage the plant's productivity. Women and children would have harvested the bulbs in the early spring and then either baked them in underground pits to be eaten immediately or dried them for winter provisions. The First

Nations communities were still harvesting camas in the early 1900s, but by the 1960s, the plant was rare.

JB wants to change this. He has mapped out a few areas where the blue flowers still grow and soon planned to harvest some. He also started a small garden at a local school where he is growing camas that one day will be ready to eat too. He's not the only one planning to taste the queen root for the first time. Across the Island, numerous food-revival projects are reclaiming the traditions of the past, and camas is of great interest.

Nancy Turner is a professor in the School of Environmental Studies at the University of Victoria, and JB has learned a lot from her. Turner has spent decades studying the traditional foods of the First Nations peoples on Vancouver Island. "Some foods, you can pinpoint exactly when they were lost," she said. "We have four generations over which camas was lost." But she's hopeful that this recent interest in edible native species will bring the foods back. She even imagines all of Canadian society enjoying these wild plants. "There are some wonderful foods out there," she said. "Every different food has a different potential. I would like to see a lot more of them grown in people's yards and gardens. I grow a lot of blueberries and huckleberries. I have camas and wild onions. They can be a specialty food, add new and different flavourings. We are never going to go back to eating exclusively saskatoon berries and bison, but we can do a lot better than what we have done with the things growing around here."

Turner is not alone in believing that a Canadian diet in the future should include more wild foods people here have forgotten how to eat. The Centre for Non-Timber Resources, a research centre at Royal Roads University in Sooke dedicated to the sustainable use of forest products, holds that a component of a local food economy is wild foods that have a monetary worth of more than $1 billion. The list is extensive and includes wild mushrooms, saskatoon berries and native nuts such as hickory, butternut, beechnuts, North American chestnuts and native hazelnuts.

Imagine not needing to buy lemons because we could get that flavour from Grand Fir instead. JB offered me some wild onion, a thin chive-like plant that to me tasted like a good vichyssoise soup. Ever since, I've been curious to learn about other unexpected foods that grow outside my house. I've been eating greens like lamb's quarters that most of us call weeds, steaming them or adding them to a salad. I have my eye on a scraggly plant that grows out of the cracks in the pavement; it's called a pineapple plant and I hear it makes a great tea. This could be a culinary adventure that opens the taste buds of our entire society and reclaims parts of a lost culture.

Turner is hopeful that we'll come around to our indigenous foods. "Don't assume that because these foods aren't being used right now, that they will not be used in the future," she said. "I can see in one hundred years people looking back and thinking 'Those poor people. They didn't have these foods. Now people are eating them all the time.'"

．　．　．

The other day I received an email from Brenda Hsueh. She's the former Bay Street employee and farm intern I met at Everdale Organic Farm and Environmental Learning Centre on a cold fall morning when she was out in the fields picking beets. Brenda wanted to be a farmer and was hoping to sell her condominium in downtown Toronto so she could purchase a farm. The email was a happy one. She had bought her farm. She was taking possession of the property in Grey County in time to get a first crop in the ground. Her goal was to sell organic vegetables at the farmers' market come summer. Then, a few days later, I spoke with SPIN farmer Jean Snow out in Dartmouth, Nova Scotia. She told me she would be tripling the number of gardens to cultivate that summer. She was excited. When I spoke to Greg Gerrits on Elmridge Farm in the Annapolis Valley, he had his crops in the ground already, and Donald Daigle out in New Brunswick told me he and his son were actively looking at farms for sale because they are considering going into cranberry production together. Later in the spring, Simon-Pierre Bolduc called from Fromagerie La Station and told me that their Alfred Le Fermier had won three prizes at Quebec's prestigious Caseus cheese awards.

I was thrilled to hear all this good news. Despite the hurdles for young farmers, younger people are buying farms. Despite how hard it can be to make a living in agriculture, the number of farmers continues to grow. Even though a truly sustainable and local food system here in Canada may still be a distant reality, the more that people like those I met while writing this book continue their good work, the more likely it is that such a system will one day exist.

We don't really know what's in store for us—we don't know what the system that Harriet Friedmann would call the third food regime will look like. In 2001, academics Tim Lang and Michael Heasman coined the term "food wars" in their book of the same name. They argued that the tension along the food chain from farmer to producer to retailer to consumer is the result of friction between different visions for how food should be produced and marketed in the future. These tensions exist between those who want to preserve the status quo of industrially produced foods, supermarkets and global chains and the people who support a new order in which food democracy reigns and where people have greater control over what they eat. Tom Henry on his farm in Metchosin holds a similar opinion. He sees a faceoff between the mainstream and the alternative. "I often describe it as two opposing forces," he said, "one of which is the farm crisis and the other is the local interest in sustainable food. I say it's a race, and the outcome is by no means obvious."

•

There's a saying in the local-food movement that in making different food choices, we are voting with our forks. The analogy to the democratic process is taken one step further with the concept Lang and Heasman describe as a food democracy, a system in which eaters have more control. With this in mind, I've come up with a list to help us make the food choices that can push us towards a better system. I'm not a local-food perfectionist. I still fumble around at the grocery store. But I do feel more confident in my choices the more I learn about how food is produced in Canada and the direction in which I think agriculture and food production should be headed. These are the rules I live by:

1. Ask questions. I try to find out where foods come from and how they are grown, both at the farmers' market and the grocery store. My kids aren't old enough to be embarrassed by me yet, so I ask lots of questions, including: Where does this food come from? What can you tell me about the way it was produced? Were these carrots delivered directly to the store, or did they pass through a distribution centre?

2. Buy foods grown on farms practising sustainable farming. Is the farm certified organic? Ask if the farm uses pesticides and herbicides. If the answer is yes, do they practise integrated pest management (IPM), a system that reduces the amount of chemicals used on fields? How do they fertilize their fields? If they say they grow sustainably, ask them to explain.

3. Eat in season. Choose local fruits and vegetables as they come into season. Instead of eating asparagus all year round, buy local produce in the spring. Skip the air-freighted Chilean raspberries and wait for local berries in July. And forget about those Chinese snow peas—fresh local ones are so much tastier. In the winter, explore root vegetables and squashes, and find out what nearby greenhouses are producing in an ecological way. I find that my family has a more varied diet when we eat this way because I am constantly adapting the dishes I cook to suit the season.

4. Avoid processed foods. You can phone company headquarters to find out where they sourced the palm oil listed in the ingredients. But better yet, cook your own meals from scratch. It's cheaper (organic ingredients for a lasagna will cost you less than a frozen entrée) and healthier (you can control sodium and fat levels). And making dinner doesn't have to be a major undertaking. To minimize my time in the kitchen, I use a slow cooker, bake in large batches to freeze, and make simple meals when I don't have time to cook.

5. Choose organic and humanely raised meats, dairy and eggs. If you are trying to minimize your carbon footprint, meat and dairy is a good place to start, considering the ecological impact of livestock and dairy production. Ask if the cattle lived on a feedlot and whether they were fed a diet free of animal by-products. How much time did the chickens or dairy cattle spend outside? Were the pigs raised in an industrial-scale barn? How many hogs were kept in one pen? How big was the pen? Were the animals given antibiotics? Humanely raised meat is generally a lot more expensive than your average supermarket cuts. In our family, we compensate for the higher prices by cooking with meat less often—about twice a week.

6. Voice your opinion. Tell your grocer that you want to buy local potatoes, not imported Parisian-cut ones from Idaho. If they don't bring in the potatoes you want, then consider changing grocers. If you can't switch, then start a conversation with the produce manager and explain why buying from local farmers is good for both business and the planet.

7. Go to the source. You will be able to find out more about how your food is produced if you get as close to the source as possible. If you purchase half a lamb or a twenty-kilogram bag of organic potatoes directly from the farmer, you will save money *and* support local agriculture—with the added bonus of not needing to go grocery shopping as frequently, though you do need space for your stores. Numerous online resources can help you find farmers in your area.

8. Look for restaurants where local and sustainable food is served. Ask the waiter how the meat was raised, where the eggs come from and whether the restaurant buys directly from farmers. Always ask if a dish (or sauce, dressing or soup) is made from scratch. Tell the person behind the counter in the food court that you'd prefer to buy a sandwich or pad Thai that is made from fresh, local ingredients.

9. Search out the alternative. If you can't find what you want at the supermarket, a community-supported agriculture plan might suit your needs, or perhaps a different store sells what you are looking for. The Internet is your friend in helping to locate what you want. The local-food movement is active across the country, in both rural areas and in small and large cities alike. Many alternatives exist if you hunt them down.

10. Choose fair trade. When you do buy imports, choose organic and fair trade products such as shade-grown, bird-friendly coffee or organic bananas so our purchases help to produce an Earth-friendly, people-friendly food system abroad as well as at home.

Of course, there are many things you can do to support the creation of a new local food system, like helping out at a community food centre, volunteering with a fruit-gleaning project, planting a vegetable garden and voting for political candidates who support a new food economy.

I often remember how Harriet Friedmann compared the new shoots of an alternative food system to dandelions. We were in a Toronto subway station, and my train was thundering through the tunnel towards us. We had been discussing all the different ways people were finding to access local food, to get around the system and find what they really wanted to eat. "Dandelions are the first plants to come back and break up the concrete. The trees, they come after that. All these little experiments are the cracks in the sidewalk, making way for a whole new ecology," she said.

If these dandelions are so impressive, then imagine what the trees will be like.

ACKNOWLEDGEMENTS

'd like to thank the hundreds of people who helped me along the way. I interviewed so many interesting and knowledgeable people—farmers, gardeners, cheese makers, friends, chefs, researchers, academics, activists, foodies of all sorts—that it would be impossible to name everybody here. But your help, expertise, stories and insights were invaluable and made this book what it is.

A big thank you to all those who fed me, who welcomed me into their homes and showed me such wonderful hospitality, including: Donald and Viola Daigle, Greg and Suzanne Gerrits, Rupert Jannasch, Mary Alice Johnson, Sinclair Philip and the many chefs who wanted me to taste the magic they make with Canadian foods; thanks also to chefs Dawn Woodward and Ed Rek, who shared their behind-the-scenes knowledge. Academics Tony Fuller, Harriet Friedmann and Keith Mullinix allowed me to hitch a ride on their years of academic study and share in their expertise—and enjoy some great conversations too.

It was a pleasure and an honour to work with editor Jim Gifford, whose insight helped to shape the book. Thank you to Kate Cassaday, who also provided great feedback, as well as to Shaun Oakey for his exactitude. It's been superb to work with devoted locavore Rob Firing. And thank you to my agent, Margaret Hart.

Thanks to the Knight Science Journalism Fellowships at MIT for inviting me to their Food Boot Camp, where I had the opportunity to learn even more about food in North America.

I'd also like to thank my friends who encouraged me, including the most vociferous cheerleaders: Piali Roy for too much to list, as well as Shahnaz Khan and Ameena Sultan. Thank you to Sarmishta Subramanian for help at the proposal stage and to Sarah Gower for editorial comments; also to Michael and Nicole Keating for their organizational brilliance.

Writing a book, I've learned, is a family affair. My profound gratitude to my parents, Jacqueline and Peter, for babysitting, logistical and meal support, grammatical thoughts, as well as their love and encouragement; and to Amtu and Nurdin for keeping us nourished with fabulous food and company. To my sister, Elyssa, for her unfailing belief in me and her science brain, and to Paul for sharing his savvy. Thanks to Jo-Ann and Hugh Robertson for their ecological leadership and to Hugh for his helpful notes and comments. Thank you to Anisa and Nadia for being so much fun and great eaters too. And thanks to my grandmother Marjorie Abrams, whose sharp mind and good company I miss tremendously, for unknowingly supporting this endeavour; she would have been the first to buy a copy.

The biggest thanks of all to Kumail: without your love and support, this would never have happened.

APPENDIX

ORGANIZATIONS: Groups working in Canada to build local food systems and to support a gastronomy of place.

National:
Slow Food Canada *www.slowfood.ca*
MetroAg Alliance for Urban Agriculture *www.metroagalliance.org*
City Farmer *www.cityfarmer.org*
Beyond Factory Farming *http://beyondfactoryfarming.org*
Canadian Organic Growers *www.cog.ca*
Compost Council of Canada *www.compost.org*
Food Secure Canada *http://foodsecurecanada.org*
Seeds of Diversity *www.seeds.ca*

Regional:
Atlantic Canadian Organic Regional Network *www.acornorganic.org*
CHEP, Good Food Incorporated *www.chep.org*
Ecology Action Centre *www.ecologyaction.ca*
Équiterre *www.equiterre.org*

Farm Folk/City Folk *www.ffcf.bc.ca*

Food Down the Road *www.fooddowntheroad.ca*

Food Matters Manitoba
   http://food.cimnet.ca/cim/43C1_3T1T4T1034.dhtm

Food Security Network of Newfoundland and Labrador
   www.foodsecuritynews.com

FoodShare Toronto *www.foodshare.net*

Growing Food Security in Alberta *www.foodsecurityalberta.ca*

Island Chefs' Collaborative *www.iccbc.ca*

Just Food *www.justfood.ca*

LifeCycles Project *http://lifecyclesproject.ca*

Local Food Plus *www.localfoodplus.ca*

Not Far from the Tree *www.notfarfromthetree.org*

The Rooftop Garden Project *www.rooftopgardens.ca*

The Stop Community Food Centre *www.thestop.org*

PEI Food Security Network *http://peifoodsecurity.wordpress.com*

Toronto Food Policy Council *www.toronto.ca/health/tfpc_index.htm*

Vancouver Food Policy Council
   http://vancouver.ca/commsvcs/socialplanning/initiatives/foodpolicy

Yukon Food *www.yukonfood.com*

FARMER EDUCATION AND INTERNSHIPS

Collaborative Regional Alliance for Farmer Training in Ontario
   www.craftontario.ca

Everdale Organic Farm and Environmental Learning Centre
   www.everdale.org

Falls Brook Centre *www.fallsbrookcentre.ca*

FarmStart *www.farmstart.ca*

Soil, Canada's Sustainable Farm Apprenticeship Program
   www.soilapprenticeships.org

World Wide Opportunities on Organic Farms *http://wwoof.ca*

FARMERS' MARKETS, CSAS AND OTHER WAYS OF PROCURING LOCAL FOOD

Eat Well Guide *www.eatwellguide.org*

Farmers' Markets Canada *www.farmersmarketscanada.ca*

Niagara Local Food Coop *www.niagaralocalfoodcoop.ca*

Ontario CSA Directory *http://csafarms.ca/index.html*

Ottawa Valley Food Co-operative *www.ottawavalleyfood.org*

Really Local Harvest Cooperative *www.recoltedecheznous.com*

ENDNOTES

INTRODUCTION

1 Mario Giampietro and David Pimentel, "The Tightening Conflict: Population, Energy Use, and the Ecology of Agriculture," NPG Forum Series (October 1993), www.npg.org/forum_series/ tightening_conflict.htm (accessed March 2009).

2 David and Marcia Pimentel, "Land, Energy and Water: The Constraints Governing Ideal U.S. Population Size," NPG Forum Series (January 1995), www.npg.org/forum_series/land_ energy&water.htm (accessed March 2009).

3 Pimentel, "Land, Energy and Water."

CHAPTER ONE

4 National Farmers Union, "The Farm Crisis and Corporate Profits" (November 30, 2005), www.nfu.ca/briefs/2005/corporate_profits.pdf (accessed September 2008).

5 Farmers across the country told me similar stories of contracts being breached with impunity by large food companies. In most of these cases, the farmers had little recourse, particularly if they

hoped to secure another contract in the future. According to Darrin Qualman, director of research for the National Farmers Union, "You can't really have fair and equitable contracting if you have a significant imbalance in power. If one party has all the power and the other one doesn't, the contract becomes a legal document to enforce penalties on the weaker party."

CHAPTER TWO

6 Much of the food we eat that is grown in Canada is picked by men and women from places like Mexico, the Caribbean and the Philippines whom the Canadian government allow into this country to work on farms. Although many of these workers return to Canada year after year, they have limited rights here, are not eligible for benefits like Employment Insurance (a fund to which they contribute), and are vulnerable to abuse and exploitation. According to Chris Ramsaroop of the organization Justicia for Migrant Workers, when workers are injured on the job, typically they are sent home and often excluded from the work program in the future. A healthy local food system must function without taking advantage of farm workers from poorer countries who are desperate for work and security.

7 You can read more about the costs of industrial agriculture in Canada in Stuart Laidlaw's *Secret Ingredients: The Brave New World of Industrial Farming*.

CHAPTER THREE

8 Brian Halweil, "Grain Harvest Sets Record, But Supplies Still Tight," Vital Signs, WorldWatch Institute (December 12, 2007), www.worldwatch.org/node/5539 (accessed November 2009).

9 According to the Fertilizer Institute, a lobby group, the cost of natural gas accounts for 90 percent of the cost of producing

nitrogen fertilizer. When the price of natural gas rises, fertilizer plants often cease operation. The group is therefore advocating for the use of other fuels such as coal to make agricultural fertilizer.

10 For an example, see Environment Canada, "Connections: Canadian Lifestyle Choices and the Environment," State of the Environment Fact Sheet No. 95–1, www.ec.gc.ca/soer-ree/English/products/factsheets/95–1.cfm (accessed January 2009).

11 Niels Jungbluth, "Environmental Impacts of Food Purchases Investigated in a Modular LCA," International Conference on Ecobalance and LCA, www.esu-services.ch/download/jungbluth-india-02-food.pdf (accessed January 2009).

12 The WWF arrived at these figures by subtracting agricultural exports from agricultural production and then adding all food imports. The final figure represents the environmental footprint, expressed as the area needed to produce the amount of food we consume.

13 Dr. Mae-Wan Ho and Lim Li Ching, "Mitigating Climate Change through Organic Agriculture and Localized Food Systems," Institute of Science in Society, www.i-sis.org.uk/mitigatingClimateChange.php (accessed March 2009).

CHAPTER FIVE

14 Millennium Ecosystem Assessment, "Ecosystems and Human Well-being" (Washington, D.C.: Island Press, 2005), www.millenniumassessment.org/documents/document.356.aspx.pdf (accessed October 2008).

15 Anne C. Bellows, Katherine Brown and Jac Smit, "Health Benefits of Urban Agriculture," Community Food Security Coalition's North American Initiative on Urban Agriculture, www.foodsecurity.org/UAHealthArticle.pdf (accessed February 2009).

CHAPTER SEVEN

16 Today in North America, most cattle—both dairy and beef—are fed a diet of grains, primarily corn, a substance their stomachs are not biologically able to digest. This means cows that are fed grains rather than grass are often, if not always, sick. To ensure cows don't die prematurely from their diet of grain, many farmers use prophylactic antibiotics. For an excellent critique of this system, I recommend Michael Pollan's book *The Omnivore's Dilemma*.

SELECTED
BIBLIOGRAPHY

Journal articles are cited only in the endnotes.

Dairy Bureau of Canada. *Fundamentals of Canadian Cheese and Their Use in Fine Cuisine*. Montreal: Éditions de la Chenelière, 1992.

Davis, Mike. *Planet of Slums*. London: Verso, 1996.

Desloges, Yvon, and Marc Lafrance. *A Taste of History: The Origins of Quebec's Gastronomy*. Canada: Les Éditions de la Chenelière and Environment Canada, Canadian Parks Service, 1989.

Duncan, Dorothy. *Food, Fellowship, and Folklore, Canadians at Table: A Culinary History of Canada*. Toronto: Dundurn Press, 2006.

Ferrières, Madeleine. *Sacred Cow, Mad Cow: A History of Food Fears*. New York: Columbia University Press, 2006.

Fuller, Tony, ed. *Farming and the Rural Community in Ontario: An Introduction*. Toronto: Federation for Rural Living, 1985.

Giangrande, Carole. *Down to Earth: The Crisis in Canadian Farming*. Toronto: Anansi, 1985.

Gray, James H. *Men Against the Desert*. Saskatoon: Fifth House Publishers, 1967, 1996.

Kuyek, Devlin. *Good Crop/Bad Crop: Seed Politics and the Future of Food in Canada*. Toronto: Between the Lines, 2007.

Laidlaw, Stuart. *Secret Ingredients: The Brave New World of Industrial Farming*. Toronto: McClelland and Stewart, 2003.

Levenstein, Harvey. *Paradox of Plenty: A Social History of Eating in Modern America*. New York: Oxford University Press, 1993.

———. *Revolution at the Table: The Transformation of the American Diet.* New York: Oxford University Press, 1988.

Menzies, Heather. *By the Labour of their Hands: The Story of Ontario Cheddar Cheese*. Kingston: Quarry Press, 1994.

Montgomery, David R. *Dirt: The Erosion of Civilizations*. Berkeley: University of California Press, 2007.

Pfeiffer, Dale Allen. *Eating Fossil Fuels: Oil, Food and the Coming Crisis in Agriculture*. Gabriola Island, B.C.: New Society Publishers, 2006.

Pollan, Michael. *The Omnivore's Dilemma: A Natural History of Four Meals*. New York: Penguin, 2006.

Strange, Marty. *Family Farming: A New Economic Vision*. Lincoln: University of Nebraska Press, 1988.

Trubeck, Amy B. *Haute Cuisine: How the French Invented the Culinary Profession*. Philadelphia: University of Pennsylvania Press, 2000.

Van der Ploeg, Jan Douwe. *The New Peasantries*. London: Earthscan, 2008.

Wilford, Allen. *Farm Gate Defense*. Toronto: New Canada Publications, 1985.

Winson, Anthony. *The Intimate Commodity: Food and the Development of the Agro-Industrial Complex in Canada*. Toronto: Garamond Press, 1993.

Woods, Nancy, and Arete Swartz Warren. *Glass Houses: A History of Greenhouses, Orangeries and Conservatories*. London: Aurum Press, 1988.

INDEX

Locavore is printed on Ancient Forest Friendly paper,
made with 100% post-consumer waste.